Paths to Recovery for Gay and Bisexual Drug Addicts

Paths to Recovery for Gay and Bisexual Drug Addicts

Healing Weary Hearts

Paul Schulte

ROWMAN & LITTLEFIELD
Lanham • Boulder • New York • London

Published by Rowman & Littlefield
A wholly owned subsidiary of The Rowman & Littlefield Publishing Group, Inc.
4501 Forbes Boulevard, Suite 200, Lanham, Maryland 20706
www.rowman.com

Unit A, Whitacre Mews, 26-34 Stannary Street, London SE11 4AB

British Library Cataloguing in Publication Information Available

Library of Congress Control Number: 2015935634

ISBN: 978-1-4422-4998-1 (cloth : alk. paper) ISBN: 978-1-4422-4999-8 (electronic)

™ The paper used in this publication meets the minimum requirements of American National Standard for Information Sciences—Permanence of Paper for Printed Library Materials, ANSI/NISO Z39.48-1992.

Printed in the United States of America

To all Gay and Bisexual Men:
Being insincere is exhausting.
May you seek authenticity!

"When the world within us is destroyed and becomes a lost and ruined self; when it is dead and loveless; and when we are in helpless despair, that is when we can re-create our world anew! We can re-assemble the pieces and infuse life into dead fragments."

—Hanna Segal, *A Psycho-Analytical Approach to Aesthetics*

Contents

Acknowledgments

This book is ten years in the making. In 2005, I enrolled in a program in drug and alcohol counseling at a West Coast university. I was lucky enough to do my internship at a program housed in a prestigious school of medicine. While there, I was able to see firsthand the many programs that have been implemented to help the gay community cope with this plague called crystal methamphetamine (hereafter CMA). Since then, I have worked in many different ways with hundreds of gay, bisexual, and straight men on three continents who are seeking recovery from drug and alcohol addiction. I am very grateful to professionals in the field, including the tireless Dr. Steve Shoptaw, Sherry Larkins, Jack Kearney, and Barry Cardiner. I am especially grateful to Dr. Steve Shoptaw for allowing me to use some of the data from the unpublished study on gay men who were treated for CMA use. Other people who have been helpful to me include Kendall Law, Philip Eisenbeiss, Simon Page, Alastair Hudson, Peter Dung, Chris Mikosh, Annabel Betz, Vince Turcotte, Tim Bush, Brian Ganson, and Elizabeth Pisani. I am especially grateful to Bill Fulco, PhD, who has blazed a multidecade trail in the treatment of addicts in Los Angeles. Special thanks go to my agent Scott Edelstein and the wonderful editor Cathy Broberg, and special thanks to Amy King who gave me the courage to write this book and who helped form its contents.

Introduction

Addiction: A Disease of Family, Perception, Loneliness, and Secrets

I am gay and I come from a family that is plagued by the disease of alcoholism. Two family members have died of complications from this disease. My father died in 1990 when I was twenty-six and my brother died five years later when he was just forty-five. As with other alcoholic families, mine did not seem to provide much room for either fairness or grief. Alcoholics die young for no good reason. Their deaths are needless. In alcoholic families, the process of grieving and letting go of members who have died of alcoholism is usually short-circuited or made impossible altogether by dousing any dangling emotion with, what else, alcohol. In other words, the time and space allowed for grieving is practically nonexistent, since alcohol is an all-purpose "depressant" for emotions. Emotions are "pressed down," "depressed," truncated and shut away in a secret and shameful box and left in some cobweb-filled mental attic. These boxes, however, rattle away in the early hours of the morning. These boxes of tangled, corroded emotions keep rattling away and the soul cries out for the release found through the grieving process. People need to be allowed to take down the boxes, open them in a safe place and say in a loud and clear voice, "This happened to me!" as many times as is necessary until the past is reconciled and forgiveness of self and others is achieved. This is what sobriety is about.

We need to undergo the process of grieving when we lose anything of significance in our lives: a childhood, innocence, distant fathers, heterosexual "normality," a "regular" upbringing, or a home where there are solid examples of leadership, love, and wisdom. And we need a grieving process for someone near to us who has died an alcoholic death. More than a decade after my father's and brother's untimely deaths, I still had not resolved the loss in my mind (I locked the attic and lacked the courage to explore the rattling). I eventually enrolled in a drug and alcohol counseling program to learn more about the disease that has haunted my family—and me—for decades. I studied the fundamentals of addiction and how it affects the body, brain, and spirit. And I studied how it causes a toxic enmeshment of the family unit and destroys normal boundaries in twisted and tormenting ways. In time, I would learn that, at its heart, recovery from drugs and alcohol is actually a grieving process for four main losses: the loss of family structures; the loss of a "normal" perspective on life; the loss of the ability to connect with people; and the loss of a world with no secrets and shame.

As part of this program, I completed an internship at UCLA where I witnessed the specific ways that the gay community has been plagued by addiction, especially in the area of crystal meth, and learned of the unique challenges gay and bisexual people face as they try to remove themselves from addiction's death grip. I saw that the gay or bisexual man enters the painful odyssey of alcoholism with an additional and heightened level of secrets, resentments, and feelings of unworthiness, shame, and remorse. These feelings of apartness that are more magnified and intense than for the average heterosexual alcoholic. And I learned that the gay community has been ravaged by addiction at a rate which is about two to three times higher than the heterosexual population.[1]

I recognized that alcoholism is a way out of the alienation of the gay or bisexual person's divided self since alcohol or drugs quiet the conflicted and shame-filled self and allow escape into a pain-free fantasy land where there is no judgment from disappointed parents, no condemnation from churches, no shame about promiscuity and no recollection about the ever-present specter of HIV. At a certain point, however, the addiction takes over and destroys careers, relationships, family and health. In fact, "In eighteen published studies that were identified, the odds of substance use for gay and bisexual youth were . . . 190 percent higher than for heterosexual youth and . . . were 340 percent higher for bisexual youth. . . . Long-term substance use outcomes in LGB youth remain largely unknown."[2]

This book is about these 'long-term substance abuse outcomes' mentioned above. It is about loss, struggle, and grieving amid alcoholism and addiction, especially addiction to CMA. There are many paths that lead to recovery for millions of gay and bisexual men around the world who are hit disproportionately hard by the disease of alcoholism. Although much of the material will apply to anyone dealing with this debilitating disease, my specific focus is on the journey of the gay or bisexual man.

One chilling article referred to young people who are gay or bisexual as having a "spoiled identity," as they must cope with the stigma of their sexual orientation that essentially blemishes their character. Their very identity is considered "off" or "not quite right." This article lays out the experience in grim and depressing detail, using words that are so common in medical journals of the past ten years or so that they are almost a cliché:

> Homophobia puts many lesbian, gay and bisexual youth at risk for suicide, chemical abuse, dropping out of school, verbal and physical abuse, homelessness, prostitution, HIV infection, and psychosocial developmental delays.[3]

This book is about how we can prevent young adults from having to endure this path without opting out of life—literally and figuratively. It is also about how gay and bisexual adult men in recovery (those noble weary hearts that have seen so much death and discrimination) can heal from the scars of early abuse, HIV/AIDS trauma, stigmatization, victimization, and discrimination. Moreover, it addresses ways that they can deal with the homophobia of family, society, and church as well as their own internalized homophobia. And it is also about young men and women today (gay or bisexual and white, Latino, and African American) in their twenties and thirties who are dealing with these same issues in a freer and more accepting environment but who still deal with PTSD, crystal meth addiction, alienation from the self and the family, and an absence of heroes or mentors to guide them through difficult times. This book is about how to stay clean from substance abuse as moral, psychological, physical and childhood wounds are healed.

Chapter 1 looks at the four primary losses that accompany addiction for any population and the way in which growing up only to discover one is gay can cause painful divisions within the self. I will show how these losses and feelings of a divided self are heightened for members of the gay or bisexual community and can cause great unrecognized damage. This will offer some light on why the levels of addiction are so high in the gay and bisexual community.

The downside of this desire to escape the chaos or fear and alienation through drugs such as CMA will be discussed in chapter 2. We will discuss the results of an unpublished death study to see if and how some men who entered a CMA treatment facility died. Indeed, nine of 110 did die. The results of the study are discussed. The Four Horsemen of the CMA apocalypse are delusionality, derangement, disease, and depression. We need to add a host of other life-altering consequences including tooth decay, unemployment, HIV, heart trouble, and criminality. This chapter will catalog the tragic journey or more than 100 addicts in treatment and see what happened to them. We will examine who lived and who died—and why. Co-occurring disorders like bipolar disorder play a big role here.

In chapter 3, we will extend this journey into the "down low" bisexual male and see that in many ways, a bisexual male is not a spy but a double agent. The gay 'spy' is one who will be expelled if he is discovered. A bisexual is a kind of 'double agent' and has a more stressful existence. He is an agent acting as a spy for one group (the heterosexual population) while covertly acting on behalf of an enemy (the gay population). He is a conflicted man. If a double agent is found out, both sides feel betrayed. He hides himself because he needs to maintain his masculine role as a provider, mate, father, lover of women. Yet he has a desire for physical comfort with a man as well. We will see how this can lead to a whirlpool of shame, self-loathing, and substance abuse. And we will offer ways out.

In chapter 4, we will look at the highly sensitive and confusing world of sexual abuse and its relationship to substance abuse. The number of those in some kind of recovery from drug and alcohol abuse who self-reported that they were sexually abused as children is staggeringly high. It seems that sexual abuse is disturbingly common and yet it is treated as a taboo subject. Adult gay men who may have been sexually abused as adolescents may need to forgive themselves if they felt that they actually "liked it." We will see how important it is to find some pity for the perpetrator to forgive the behavior without excusing the behavior. Others may need to let themselves off the hook for being lost in a perpetual trap of the abuse in the way they have, as adults, revisited the childhood abuse and constructed one abusive relationship after another with other adults. Living as adults with adolescent feelings surrounding the childhood abuse—fear of being caught and its consequences, shame, and self-disgust—often leads to abusive and self-loathing behaviors in adult sexual relationships. A drug like crystal meth can sometimes block out the shame, self-loathing, and damaging memories of an abusive past. It represses the moral sense of right and wrong and allows for even deeper and more self-degrading sexual acting out. Dealing with all of this in a more open light and with an eye toward forgiveness is key.

In chapter 5, we will exit the darkness of the diagnosis and description of the plight of the gay and bisexual addict and move toward action, solutions, and agendas for recovery. When a gay man has had enough, the healing process must include three main areas of renewal: physical, emotional, and psychological. The beginning of this is recognizing that many people in the gay community—especially men over the age of forty—have experienced the deaths of people close to them by HIV-related illness. Thousands of gay men have PTSD without knowing it. Entire portions of the gay community are walking around with a chronic problem that is not diagnosed and that leads to high rates of addiction, depression, suicidality, and other life problems. Creating community awareness and a sense of heroes in the gay community is a key way out of this. Veterans can teach the gay and bisexual community something about helping each other recover from PTSD.

Chapter 6 explores how a gay or bisexual person develops a divided self and how reconciliation with this divided self can come about. It is about how gay and bisexual men can gather the strength to change and create a new set of ideals by which to live regardless of what conventional rules dictate. It is about living with authenticity.

In chapter 7, we look at the controversial topic of spirituality in recovery. Spirituality is increasingly being let into the therapist's office as a legitimate means of healing. Scientists who are dogmatic about data are reluctantly finding evidenced-based data that shows the healing power of the spiritual realm. This rapid spread of the spiritual into the therapist's room is especially difficult for many gay or bisexual men who have been expelled from (or at the very least quietly asked to leave) their religious group or have been told that their lifestyle was "corrupt," an abomination, intrinsically evil, or fundamentally wrong. As the great psychologist William James pointed in his seminal work *The Varieties of Religious Experience,* spirituality comes before religion—not the other way around. Two of the most influential psychiatrists of the twentieth century—William James and Victor Frankl—both of whom believe that hope through some form on internal spirituality is vital to mental health.

Chapter 8 is about bringing the obscure and hard to understand world of co-occurring disorders into a common language for gay and bisexual men to understand and identify. Even if in generalities, knowledge of these behaviors can go a long way toward demystifying them and removing their ability to negatively affect people. Much of this science of co-occurring disorders is new, so it is important to spread the word about current progress and connect the dots between disorders and drug use, especially to Twelve Step programs which sometimes roll their collective eyes when these topics are raised.

Chapter 9 is a call to arms. The medical/psychiatrist community has gone to one extreme of being so politically correct that it resembles a so-dependent wife who quietly reminds her husband that he should not drive drunk with the children in the car. Are their ethical obligations to raising the tone of the debate? Definitely! Yes! The shocking proliferation in CMA use and HIV transmission (especially in London and New York) in recent years is evidence that there has been a failure of imagination. It is only in its infancy in Hong Kong, for instance, and there is no plan. That goes for most Asian capitals. There is lots of heavy lifting ahead.

NOTES

1. Some studies assert that one in two gay men will at some point in their life struggle with substance abuse. The numbers through this book put the proportion of gay and bisexual men with substance abuse at about 25–35 percent. So, we need to

explore why as much as one in three of gay men have substance abuse problems. My own experience over the past twelve years of work in this area is about one in three.

2. Michael P. Marshal, Mark S. Friedman, Ron Stall, et al., "Sexual Orientation and Adolescent Substance Use: A Meta-Analysis and Methodological Review," *Addiction* 103, no 4 (2008): 546–56.

3. Arnold Grossman, "Growing Up with a 'Spoiled Identity': Lesbian, Gay and Bisexual Youth at Risk," *Journal of Gay and Lesbian Social Services* 6, no. 3 (1997): 45–56; available on Internet in 2008.

Part One

THE ALIENATED AND DIVIDED SELF OF THE GAY AND BISEXUAL MAN

Chapter One

The Four Losses of Gay Men

Family, Perception, Dignity, and Connection

THE DISEASE OF THE LOST FAMILY

My own journey is a typical page from the clichéd annals of the alcoholic family. Alcoholism is called a "disease of the family" in that it affects all of the individuals in the "alcoholic unit," albeit in slightly different ways. Children in an alcoholic family are often denied a sense of fairness and intimacy, and often lose their innocence as they are forced to parent their own alcoholic parent. As adults, some of these children long to find the "love" their alcoholic parents showed them during their childhood (in actuality, it was often verbal or physical abuse) and marry other equally abusive alcoholics. These Children of the Wrath, as I like to call them, are conditioned to see love as a series of conflicts when they are young and so they practice conflict in their adult relationships.

Children of alcoholics have often tragically learned that love means fighting, so they seek out someone who can provide the familiar conflict that was initially offered by one or both of their parents. Some children in alcoholic homes learn that love means bullying—physically or intellectually putting people down. Some of them swear that they will never grow up to be like their fathers or mothers, and yet they end up exactly like them. The "sin of Adam" is never too far away.

Others in the family take the opposite route and become a "doormat" or make themselves into a "chameleon" in order to avoid incurring the wrath of the alcoholic parent. This carries into adult life as well, with these people refusing to stand up for themselves or, for that matter, anything of importance.

Some children try to become the "good little boy" or "good little girl" and make a series of compromises to accommodate the raging parent. If they are just good enough, they mistakenly believe, their behavior can fix the problem and their home can become whole. If a boy realizes he is gay, he will go to just about any lengths to conceal this fact, especially from a raging alcoholic father. A bisexual adolescent will certainly try to hide the other part of himself or herself as well. They (rightfully) fear beatings, ridicule, groundings, or expulsion from the home. The secrets and feelings of fakery start very early and are almost hardwired by adulthood.

Through no fault of their own, children of alcoholics may also inherit the gene structure for alcoholism from their parents. The genetic pilot light under the water tank is on and it needs only a little nudge and they become a boiling cauldron of rage, resentment, depression, and self-disgust—and lots of alcohol. Though the numerous studies on this subject produce a wide range of findings, many suggest that at least 60 percent of the alcoholic's disease can be traced to the genetic roots of the family tree. Scientists may have found the precise protein responsible for this in chromosome 7, called "muscarinic acetylcholine receptor M2" (CHRM2). It presents a high risk factor for alcoholism as well as its cousin, depression. [1]

In short, if a parent or a grandparent is an alcoholic, there's a good chance the son or daughter (or grandchild) will be as well. This is, incidentally, often the source for alcoholic resentment. "I did not choose this—it was given to me in my genes." The point here is that study after study indicates that the chances of a gay or bisexual man becoming an alcoholic—independent of having an alcoholic parent—are about three to four times higher than for the heterosexual population. As we will see, the gay man carries a "gene pool" risk as well as a "sexual identity" risk from discrimination and a confused identity, which can lead to alcoholism. In another study, it was concluded that one in two gay men will struggle with some form of substance abuse in their lives. The gay community is a cauldron of alcohol and drug dependence.

THE DISEASE OF LOST PERCEPTION

Alcoholism is frequently called a "disease of perception"—a markedly similar chord in the alcoholic personality that causes the person to see himself as "less than" or as "counterfeit." We sometimes hear the words "fraudulent" when alcoholics describe their take on themselves. And this feeling of being a fraud or a fake often precedes the first drink. There is a common phrase to describe this, which is F-E-A-R: "false evidence appearing real." Addicts experience a heightened sense of fear that they will be made to look like a fool or be found out.

The alcoholic's inner sense of inferiority persists despite the total absence of evidence in the outside world. No matter the accomplishments, the degrees on the wall, or the money in the bank, the alcoholic is taunted by a compelling and gnawing voice deep down that whispers over and over again, "You are unworthy." The alcoholic mind often creates false scenarios that speak of failure, transgression, or brokenness when there is absolutely no outside confirmation of this.

Alcohol and drugs are seen as a solution because they alter that perception and, as the great philosopher William James points out, make a person "for the moment one with truth. Not through mere perversity do men run after it. . . . It stands in place of the symphony concerts and of literature."[2] Alcohol and drug use offers an alternate reality. Unfortunately, this new reality is often delusional, self-destructive, and offensive. Instead of taking adult action to change one's circumstances, the person skips that step and instead alters his perception of what he considers to be an unacceptable state of affairs. The healing in this regard comes from recognizing that alcohol had a role in altering perception when one could no longer tolerate the reality around him but could also not change it. In this way, alcohol and drugs played a positive role—until they didn't. In a world where the gay or bisexual person is seen as a criminal, a "fairy," or just "not quite one of the group," alcohol and drugs present a perfect way to escape this reality of discrimination and stigmatization. If a man who is gay is perceived as a pervert, then he is likely to act like one. If he is sidelined and stigmatized, he may end up rejecting society and forcing himself into a marginalized professional setting. He may opt for a "gay ghetto" where he feels safe, but subsequently reduces his opportunities in society.

THE DISEASE OF LOST CONNECTION

Alcoholism is a "disease of loneliness"—it causes an otherwise rational person to think that consuming vast amounts of a depressant called ethyl alcohol while sitting alone will somehow soothe the pain and provide companionship. And it's an answer that has been given much credence. For example, William James inferred that alcohol was a solution to the "bone-chilling isolation of the sick soul." He wrote that the person who feels like an "isolated sick soul" seems to have been born that way. Alcohol and drugs do offer some respite from lifelong feelings of apartness, of feeling like one is on the outside. Indeed, alcoholism is the disease of the outsider, of people who feel that they don't fit in and are somehow apart from others.

Gay or bisexual people, in particular, can feel like a stranger in their own land. I use the analogy of a double agent—the consequences of being caught or judged either by one's wife or lover can be staggering. Of course, it is even more stressful for those who live a triple life—one for the wife, one for the gay world, and one for the day-to-day world. The recovery process here involves mourning lost friendships and lost family while also recognizing that recovery can create new relationships.

There is a good analogy here. Gay people are like left-handers. Left-handers are constantly reminded of their difference because the world is built for the majority (about 85 percent) of people who are right-handed. Scissors, punch ladles, frying pans, doors, high school and university desks. On and on it goes. The same is true with gay people but in a more profound way. The legal system is built for heterosexuals. (In fact, in almost eighty countries, it is a felony to be homosexual.) The religious system is built for heterosexuals. The high school dating system is built exclusively for heterosexuals. This is true for university life, work functions, and so on. The gay person is constantly reminded that he does not quite fit in.

THE DISEASE OF LOST TRUTH
WHERE FANTASY AND SECRETS LIVE

Addiction is a "disease of secrets"—the person may do astounding and seemingly crazy things while intoxicated but can be, during the sober daytime, a respected president of a company or an admired millionaire banker. What happened the night before (especially if the person cannot even remember it) must be kept hidden at all costs. In addition, since most alcoholics come from alcoholic families, they carry a trait that was beaten into them (literally or figuratively) that everything is okay as long as it *looks okay* on the outside. The internal strife of the alcoholic family must be hidden from public view at all costs. So, the person who comes from the alcoholic family learns to keep secrets and to live in the shadows of half-truths and deception. The façade is all that counts—the rest can be made up to suit the audience. The old adage rings loud and clear here: You are as sick as your secrets. A 2013 Pew survey discovered that only 28 percent of men who identified as bisexual said they were open about it. And the American Institute for Bisexuality said that women were far more likely to express bisexuality than men.[3]

When we deal with secrets, we are dealing with something that, if discovered, would have negative or dangerous consequences—punishment, embarrassment, humiliation, and so on. Addicts often associate secrets with something that was done to them, which makes them a victim. As victims, they feel justified anger, resentment, bitterness, or revenge. All of these are poisonous emotions to which the addict feels entitled. They own them because they earned them. Bill Wilson, the co-founder of Alcoholics Anonymous, had a piercing insight on this subject; he said "Few people have been more victimized by resentments than have we alcoholics. . . . Anger, that occasional luxury of more balanced people . . . often lead straight to the bottle."[4] The process of recovery here involves realizing that secrets and resentments are two sides of the same coin. Freedom from secrets is possible—so is freedom from resentment.

ALCOHOLISM AND THE GAY OR BISEXUAL MAN

When we are working with a gay or bisexual man (as well as many bisexual women) who may be an addict/alcoholic, the toxic blend of behaviors described above (secrecy, loneliness, victimization, and unworthiness) is especially hazardous. This is because most gay or bisexual men carry an additional level of secrets, resentments, and feelings of unworthiness, shame, and remorse connected to their sexual orientation. The gay man often fears alienation or expulsion from the group if his secret is discovered. Furthermore, he often experiences a chasm between who he is as a sexual being and what others expect him to be. He may be haunted by the secrets of his nighttime behavior, whether it be a secret tryst or visits to a bathhouse or a public restroom. In all this covert activity, there is often the resentful and sad refrain, "Why did you make me this way, God?" Of course, we have come a long way in terms of acceptance but, as we will see in this book, current data do not show a corresponding decrease in drug and alcohol problems within the gay community. If anything, both the quantity and the danger level of drug use seems to be accelerating. Society is more supportive than ever but, as stated above, there are still "almost 80 countries which outlaw homosexuality with penalties which range from imprisonment to execution. . . . Six Islamic countries impose the death penalty (for homosexuality). In four others, lesbians and gays can be stoned to death." We sometimes need a reality check on just how far we have come.[5]

THE GAY ADDICT AND THE DISEASE OF THE LOST FAMILY

Most gay and bisexual alcoholics come from alcoholic families, where they learned to guard the secrets of abuse and neglect so common to the alcoholic home. Thus, this addict is already skilled in the art of deceiving people about the reality of his "home," presenting an outside view that differs dramatically from the truth that lies inside, when he has to add yet another level of deception. He is an inventor of reality—a reality that is befogged by myriad impressions the gay or bisexual man feels he needs to project.

He is an impressionist, a chameleon who wants to fit in. He seeks to allay his loneliness in any way he can. It is a lost self that is full of shame. The combination of coming from an alcoholic home and carrying the frequent self-hatred of being gay or bisexual may turn his sexual life into a dark and abusive odyssey of unhealthy acting out with other men that reflects his shame. It is not surprising: people who are full of shame do shameful things.

In numerous studies on gay and bisexual addiction, the medical cliché is that LGBT people often suffer from "negative life outcomes." This is due to rejection, victimization, fear of reprisal if discovered (for bisexual men especially), expulsion from the family unit, rejection by their religious communities, feelings of alienation and aloneness, suicidality, and depression. They are at high risk of alcohol and drug abuse. In many cities, the problem of drug and alcohol addiction (particularly with crystal methamphetamine [hereafter CMA]) among gays has actually accelerated in recent years, especially in London. We have come a long way, but in many ways we made only slight progress.

In the absence of support from the family, especially an understanding father, many gay and bisexual men struggle to find heroes, values, and a framework from which to grow and flourish. This produces an array of profound effects on the whole of gay men who are trying to form a community:

1. They do not know what is central to their lifestyle.
2. They have few guideposts to help organize a sexual relationship.
3. They often feel painted into a corner where they choose to create a counterfeit façade to please society.
4. They wander around in the darkness when it comes to their own sexuality—and sexuality is certainly a fundamental part of what it means to be human.

This sexual part of the gay or bisexual man becomes a stranger. It is unfamiliar or even unknown. It seems too hot to touch. Ultimately, the person may discover that alcohol or other drugs allows him to get near to this emotional flame without psychic self-immolation. The sexuality often remains hidden to his own self. He skates from one anonymous sexual encounter to another. He is like a spy in a foreign land. This is the added layer of fraudulence, which is that mysterious feature of alcoholism. This is true with both gay and bisexual men. Alcoholism is a way out of the alienation of the divided self. The fraudulence and being forced to become a spy in his own land creates a combination of sadness and rage that manifests itself in many ways. Anonymous sex is a kind of aggression. Catty behavior is another. An indulgence in S&M can be another yet again.

THE GAY AND BISEXUAL EXPERIENCE OF THE DISEASE OF PERCEPTION

Alcoholics often feel like frauds or counterfeits, a tendency exacerbated for the gay man who feels this way not only when it comes to his alcohol use but when it comes to his sexuality as well—and he has ever since the first time he undressed in the locker room and had secret fantasies about the other boys around him. The natural feelings of arousal are also a source of shame and secrets. Having to avert his stares at men and pretend to like women in high school or college is difficult and reinforces the feelings of being a counterfeit. This requires a gay man to become something like a "spy" in his own land. If he is discovered, he will be punished if not physically then socially. We have, indeed, come a long way, but homophobia is never very far away. In this book we will discuss a number of studies which show that self-destruction in the gay community is alive and well.

Today we know that a substantial portion of runaways in the United States are gay or bisexual. Many have been forced from their homes because of their sexual orientation. Gay and bisexual male youth appear to be at increased risk for both homelessness and suicide. In one study, 40 percent of LGBT subjects had suicidal thoughts or actually tried to commit suicide. Young people who are coping with gay or bisexual feelings are at particular risk for suicide.[6] Furthermore, they are more likely to engage in survival sex (prostitution) than their non-gay male counterparts. Prejudice, discrimination, and homophobia are still rampant in society today; these are contributing factors to a multiplicity of problems for young gay people, in the age range of fourteen to twenty.[7]

THE GAY AND BISEXUAL EXPERIENCE AND THE DISEASE OF LONELINESS

And there is the alcoholic "disease of loneliness" compounded by a world of the gay man where the center of community activity is *still* often the bar or club. Many alcoholic men in recovery report that the loneliest place on earth was in a club with a drink in one's hand surrounded by hundreds of beautiful men. These places are teeming with alcohol, drugs, and promiscuity. While there has been great progress over the past several years in terms of cultural acceptance, the legal right to form gay unions or to marry, and in offerings of alternative forms of entertainment for gay men, the evidence of alienation, dysfunctionality, and self-loathing is still ample. We will see that HIV transmission rates are at all-time highs in London, for instance.

HIV infection is on the rise and gay men in their twenties and thirties are still are about three times more likely to experience periods of alcohol dependence compared to their heterosexual counterparts. Furthermore, crystal methamphetamine use is rampant in the gay club scene in every single gay "mecca" around the globe and is causing great damage to many lives, especially in London. The wild popularity of a book like *The Velvet Glove*—a candid and moving search for the causes of rage (active and passive) in the gay community—indicates that many gay men continue to seek some kind of reconciliation in the midst of a world of secrets, misperception, loneliness, alcohol dependence, depression, and alienation.

Alcoholism has many faces, but its main feature seems to be a disease of an alienated and divided self-trying to find some kind of unity with the world. It is a person arising from the ashes of a separated and divided self. This may be more profoundly true for the gay or bisexual alcoholic. Indeed, many things conspire to prevent the gay or bisexual addict from discovering and imagining how to find a degree of unity and reconciliation of the divided self.

THE GAY SEXUAL DIVIDED SELF AND THE DISEASE OF SECRETS

The following is one example of how a gay man can have an identity that is public and known yet also have a private identity so different that he is a virtual stranger to himself. And he must keep his dual identity a secret, which only adds to his stress.

The fundamental fear at work here is the fear of being disowned—of losing the identity I was given by my family, society, and community. As we've already discussed, many gay or bisexual youth are asked to leave their homes because of their orientation, and some religious groups have little or no tolerance for homosexuality. Being rejected from the groups or institutions that made the person who he is can produce feelings of a loss of identity and a deep fear of "being crazy." This is because my idea of who I am—a social, sexual, and intellectual self—sits squarely in my mind. So, if I become a different person because the name (and the identity) I have in the community conflicts with the idea of myself that sits squarely in my mind, can I say that I am "losing my mind" in favor of a new one? In many ways, the answer is yes.

Should a gay or bisexual person repress the new self in order to make it convenient for everyone to continue to know him as the old self? He is really of two minds here, as they say. There is one word for what this person is doing when he chooses to be two different persons rather than fully embrace the new self and express that identity. It is called evasion. He becomes a spy, which comes from the French word "espionage." Sadly, synonyms for espionage are cloak and dagger, eavesdropping, infiltration. Ask any gay or bisexual man if he ever felt forced to use these methods and he will undoubtedly say yes. This is because the gay or bisexual man has to change the way he acts in order to deceive the community and prevent that community from "finding out" about him and potentially expelling him or, at the very least, pushing him aside.

We often hear that the bisexual man fears not only rejection but also retribution from his wife if she finds out. This leads to self-destructive stress, anxiety, depression, and self-loathing. It is a dishonesty that drains the soul. Why? If I reveal my own identity, there is a decent chance that I will be "deported" or "expelled." I am discovered as a spy, engaging in espionage. I shut down and turn into a split person—an alienated self. Feelings of powerlessness, confusion, anxiety, and muted rage occupy this isolated chamber of bewilderment.

HAVE WE REALLY COME SO FAR?

If we are honest, the answer is not really. There is not one single openly gay person in the U.S. Senate. There is not one openly gay person in professional football or baseball. There are no openly gay members in professional golf, hockey, or race car driving. There was not one single openly gay U.S. athlete in the most recent Winter Olympics. There is not one single active openly gay officer in any branch of the U.S. Armed Forces. There is not one single openly gay CEO in any Fortune 100 company or any openly gay CEO of any major bank in the United States. There is not one single openly gay federal judge. There is not one single openly gay NASCAR driver. Is there one openly gay high school principal in the country? Try to find one. Indeed, we have a long way to go. The Episcopal Church appointed a gay bishop several years ago and caused a damaging schism that continues to rock this church today. Incidentally, these data points are also true in most countries in the developing world. Needless to say, in places like China, Indonesia, India, and Japan, there are few if any famous gay people who can act as mentors or role models for youth.

In the book *Alcoholics Anonymous,* Bill Wilson (an alcoholic and AA cofounder who wrote most of this Twelve Step book) refers to alienation as a feeling deep down that "we never quite belonged." Many a drug addict or alcoholic who I have counseled put it in a similar way: "I was born on the outside looking in." Add to this the feature of being gay or bisexual, and it is easy to imagine a gay or bisexual alcoholic who feels like a fractured self. The allure of the bottle or a drug like crystal meth—a way to escape and feel invincible—becomes all too attractive. It is not surprising that gay and bisexual men experience rates of substance abuse that are far higher than in the heterosexual population.

The feeling of being a fake or a spy drains the life out of the gay or bisexual man. The added fear of being "found out" adds even more stress. There is a natural fear that the life in one's "true self" is being drained away. Panic sets in when the person feels that he just does not have enough energy to keep up the façade and cope with the stress of being caught. Furthermore, the fear of being found out often causes gay or bisexual men to make themselves "indispensable" at work in order to avoid being fired. This explains the sense of loneliness and feelings of desperation and exhaustion that can set in—a sense of an inevitable "crash and burn" scenario. We can see that a gay or bisexual man filled with the shame that is frivolously dispensed by the community is often a burnout case waiting to happen.

GAY AND BISEXUAL ALCOHOLICS: LOST MEN IN SEARCH OF A RECONCILED IDENTITY

When we put together the phenomenon of this misplaced or misnamed person, we can see a host of feelings that can produce great confusion and fear: (1) the feelings of being a spy; (2) the sense of fraudulence; a deep-seated, gnawing, and inexplicable sensation of feeling unworthy; (3) a split self yearning for unity; and (4) a desperate sense that there is just not enough energy to keep up the façade. It is little wonder, then, that alcohol and drugs seem like a worthwhile way out. The description that I have laid out—the feeling of being a counterfeit who will be found out eventually and "expelled"—can explain why the use of drugs like crystal meth is so rampant in this mad and lonely existence. It provides a sense of well-being, euphoria, confidence, sexual prowess, empowerment, and feelings that say "I can overcome anything."

When we feel misidentified or someone calls us by the wrong name, we cry out for an identity. We feel wronged. We will use whatever we have as a means of showing ourselves. With gay men, that may be a physically strong body or a powerful libido. It may be a strong desire for creativity. Later in this book, we will explore the preponderance of gay men employed in the arts, theater, fashion, and media. As Herman Hesse put it, "Chaos demands to be recognized and experienced before letting itself be converted into a new order."

Is the chaos created by the fear, alienation, and confusion of the gay or bisexual man related to a kind of nervous but flourishing creativity? It seems so. Prior to this creativity, is this journey of discovery often accompanied by periods of alcohol abuse and drug-taking? The odds are high. We will explore this in the next chapter.

NOTES

1. J. C. Wang, A. L. Hinrichs, H. Stock, et al., "Evidence of Common and Specific Genetic Effects: Association of the Muscarinic Acetylcholine Receptor M2 (CHRM2) Gene with Alcohol Dependence and Major Depressive Syndrome," *Human Molecular Genetics* 13 (17): 1903–11.

2. W. James, *Varieties of Religious Experience*, 162. Barnes & Noble Classics. New York, 2004.

3. Benoit Denizet-Lewis, "The Scientific Quest to Prove Bisexuality Exists," *New York Times,* March 20, 2014.

4. Bill Wilson, *12 Steps and Twelve Traditions* (New York: Alcoholics Anonymous World Services), 1952.

5. Andrew Fraser, "On Trial for Being Gay," "Attitude." June 2014. In addition, in 2014, the Catholic Cardinal of Spain said that homosexuality is a "bodily deficiency" such as high blood pressure. He said that homosexuality is a "deficient way of manifesting sexuality." He said that is it "possible to recover from homosexuality and become normal with the right treatment." This kind of medieval and uninformed language alienates Catholic gay men from their spiritual community, aggravates their identity crisis, reinforces discrimination and flies in the face of modern thinking on the topic of homosexuality. In a word, it is destructive.

6. Rita Lee, "Health Care Problems of Lesbian, Gay, Bisexual, and Transgender Patients," *Western Journal of Medicine* 172, no. 6 (June 2000): 403–408.

7. G. Kruks, "Gay and Lesbian Homeless/Street Youth: Special Issues and Concerns," *Journal of Adolescent Health* 12, no. 7 (November 1991): 515–18.

Chapter Two

Gay and Bisexual Polydrug Takers—The Living and the Dead

It is often said that by the time an alcoholic took his first drink, he needed it. An alcoholic personality wracked by morbid scruples, guilt, shame, low self-esteem and a sense of impending doom needs a drink. Or at least he thinks that a drink will quell the voices, the fears, the shame and the painful memories. I believe it is fair to say that by the time crystal methamphetamine began to spread into the gay scene in the early to mid 1990s, the gay community was ready for it—and needed it. It seemed like a perfect remedy to a catastrophic perfect storm: (1) rejection by family, church, or community and the resulting shame and guilt about being gay; (2) discrimination at work and often the fear of being fired if one's homosexuality was discovered; and (3) a devastating plague which had been wiping out a generation of talented gay singers, artists, producers, writers, playwrights and tens of thousands of regular gay and bisexual men who were decent, law-abiding citizens.

How could a drug which is as insidious and nauseating as CMA take hold and spread like wildfire in the gay community (and is still doing so today). How could something made from various cooked combinations of automobile brake fluid, industrial detergent and cough syrup prove so popular? How could something that is commonly known to cause brain damage, psychosis, and acute paranoia spread so easily? The complaint of the person seeking out a remedy through the use of CMA must be deeply painful. What kind of connection would a man want who would knowingly put his brain at risk?

If we reflect for a moment, we can see just how easy it was for this drug to spread throughout the community. A gay man in 1985 or 1990 who was around the age of twenty-five and forty-five would have seen multiple friends, sex partners, or lovers die near them or in their arms from a disease which many in society thought was just desserts for perverted homosexual activity. It was not passive disinterest. It was a clear active disgust among many people who condemned the gay community. Many friends of mine at that time who told their families that they were gay were met with well-meaning but ham-fisted responses like, "Please don't die" or "I hope you are not sick." That was the beginning and the end of the conversation. Imagine that young man who has carried around those private experiences and thoughts for decades and has nowhere to put them and no one with whom to process them.

The gay or bisexual men who used CMA were looking for two things: a connection and an escape. They wanted a connection offered by CMA which many describe as a powerful feeling of falling in love—of finally 'being understood.' It was a total release from shame and all of the worry of HIV, tragic memories about HIV or memories of early abuse. It allowed an escape in sex from the constant nagging fear of HIV transmission. It was an escape of feelings of daily fear from being found out, being fired, or being asked to leave the group. We will see how this justifiable use of the drug made perfect sense. The rapid spread of CMA occurred in the context of a gay community with deep trauma after watching a large segment of its own group die like flies. Dare we say that a justifiable diagnosis of "mass untreated Post Traumatic Stress Disorder (PTSD) was appropriate for those gay and bisexual men who were active in the gay community of metropolitan cities in the United States.

This is on top of frequent bullying, police harassment, rejection from a church community, expulsion from the family unit, and a general mistreatment by society. (In the 1980s, I had a Top Secret clearance at the White House and I clearly ran the risk of having my clearance revoked with my job being taken away had it become known that I was gay. I lived with that fear every day.)

CMA is a high-risk drug. It is perhaps one of the riskiest drugs ever invented by man. And, it is being used by more than four million Americans. It is rampant in the gay community. As of this writing, it is sweeping onto the shores of the Hong Kong and Singapore gay community at flank speed. The severity of the drug must match the severity of the complaint for the drug. Despite all the progress we have made, gay men continue to live lives of stress, anxiety, abuse, shame, and self-loathing. Their desire to escape using such an insidious drug must be profound for they do know the consequences. It is a drug for sex, indeed. But its powers to allow a gay or bisexual man to leave behind the fear, shame, self-loathing and anxiety are magical. In addition, it also allows the man to escape "HIV fatigue" (the realization that every sexual encounter with another man has the potential to kill me or at least cause me to contract a life-long chronic condition for which there is no cure and which costs thousands of dollars each year for treatment). This is also an undoubted motivator to use CMA.

Lastly, in a world dominated by youth, looks, and thin waist lines, CMA allows an aging gay man to look thin (CMA acts as an appetite suppressant and offers great energy). It allows him to feel youthful—at least at first. It allows him to blend into a youthful world of partying and the club scene. He can feel young and hip. He can indulge his Peter Pan fantasies. He can be powerful and suppress his rage. He can forget about twenty years of the "day in and day out" potential of contracting HIV. He can escape the shame and feelings of helplessness as an often oppressed minority.

We need to lay out all of these alleged benefits of this drug (often called 'pure evil') or the rest of the chapter will make no sense. We will describe in this chapter the lives of more than 100 gay and bisexual men whose careers were torpedoed, whose lives were destroyed and, in a few cases, who actually died from consequences of this drug. The astounding damage from this drug—and the depths of degradation—can only make sense in the context of all of the false promises described above: (1) a connection and what feels like true love in the arms of another man (and the chasing of this feeling in subsequent binges); (2) relief from shame, guilt, anxiety, and pressure; (3) a temporary forgetting of the trauma and anxiety surrounding HIV and all its pain; (4) an escape from a mundane dead end career path; and (5) a promise of escape and excitement from the sexual hunt.

At first, the risk associated with CMA seems worth it. Then it becomes a living hell from which many have great difficulty escaping. First, we must descend into the depths of the disease to understand the pathology in order to grasp the difficulty and the challenges of getting out of the CMA bear trap. We must keep in mind the many fantasies and false promises that CMA offers—and the way in which the gay community is so heavily damaged by a cruel recent history—or it is impossible to believe the facts that will now be put forth.

This leads us to an unpublished study at a leading West Coast university that examined case histories of gay men who had completed treatment for abuse of CMA. The study, which I had the honor to catalogue in great detail, was intended to see how well these gay men were doing after completing some form of rehabilitation and treatment. Specifically, we wanted to discover if any of the men had died and, if so, how.[1]

We began by collecting data from various sources: Treatment and medical records of each man's history of meth use, quality of health, timing and status of HIV, and mental state. We looked at the medications for HIV and/or mental disorders they were taking, and tracked their HIV transmission dates (the length of time between when a person contracts HIV and the body starts developing antibodies to fight it). Self-reported physical and psychiatric problems were noted and family histories were recorded.

Further, each of the men completed an extensive history of their medical, drug, HIV, STD, psychiatric, and family drug problems. We also searched public records of death.

Then, with all of this data before us, we dug in deep and identified similarities and differences in education, drug-taking habits, family history, incidence of HIV, medications, sexual activity, timeline of addiction history, and, most important for this study, just who died and why. In all, we had clean, comprehensive, and accurate data for 110 men who had been treated for addiction to crystal methamphetamine from 2001 to 2005. This was a large enough sample to provide some coherent averages, though now a large-scale study would yield a robust set of data. We quickly learned that, of the 110 men, nine had died since receiving drug treatment. Before we get to the tragic cases of those men, let's start at the beginning and see just how CMA took over these men's lives and their responses to the subsequent problems. (The appendix includes a table summarizing the numbers.) First, however, we'll divide this group into three subgroups: men who reported they were HIV positive (62 percent); men who reported being HIV negative (30 percent), and men who had died following treatment (8 percent).

THE HIV-POSITIVE GROUP

On average, the HIV-positive men were born in 1964. As some of the oldest members of Generation X, they would be about fifty years old in 2014. These men started drinking around the same time as many young adults, approximately age seventeen—often during the last year of high school. Most in this group of gay men dropped out of college after two or three years. Their drinking continued into their mid-twenties. Then something happened.

At age twenty-seven or twenty-eight, many of these men reported having experiences that went basically like this: they were in a club dancing one night and someone said, "Try this. It will give you extra energy." For many, this was their first use of CMA. (Both the HIV-negative and HIV-positive group members reported a similar experience.) After this first use of the drug in some kind of party atmosphere—a club, a house party, or a bathhouse during sex—they were immediately hooked. By the age of twenty-nine or so, these men were HIV positive. (Interestingly, for both the living and the dead, seroconversion took two years from the time they started CMA.)

Almost all of these men were law-abiding citizens, and as a whole, the group was generally law-abiding. Only 4 percent reported of the HIV group had ever been convicted of a felony; 80 percent of them did not even smoke cigarettes. Nonetheless, the grim reality is that within about two years of taking CMA, they were HIV positive. What was the attraction of CMA? Many of them reported that taking CMA "made the shame go away." They also said it "gave them freedom," "turned them into a bottom," and "took away inhibitions." Unfortunately, the effects of CMA—the absence of social constraint, the removal of shame, and the proclivity toward bottoming—was a recipe that would soon leave them infected with the virus that causes AIDS. Only a small number of the men in the study reported trying CMA intravenously, while 100 of them admitting to practicing unsafe sex. So, we should assume that most contracted HIV through unsafe sex. Many of these men self-reported that they "probably" contracted HIV through unsafe sex.

CMA IS ABSOLUTELY A GATEWAY DRUG TO HIV TRANSMISSION

The point here is that, on average, the men first tried CMA at age twenty-seven and were infected with HIV at twenty-nine. Using CMA clearly led to the transmission of HIV. Why do we know this? The men who were HIV positive reported having unsafe sex (anal sex without condoms) 100 percent of the time. And most of these men who were HIV positive reported their sexual activity was "compulsive." Was it compulsive before or after the CMA use? There are few studies here, but the level of sexual compulsivity likely stepped up dramatically after the men began using CMA in a problematic way. Thirty-three percent of these HIV-positive men were smokers, and it is not clear whether they started before or after they were introduced to CMA. (This is double the national average). On top of these problems, 40 percent of this group of men were using CMA intravenously. And a similar number reported having hepatitis C. It is difficult to determine with certainty whether their HIV infection came from unprotected sex or from sharing needles, but it seems that the lion's share contracted the virus from unprotected sex and a minority of these infections came from needle sharing, or "slamming." This is, indeed, a perfect storm of unsafe intravenous drug use, unsafe sex, and multiple sex partners which can easily lead to HIV transmission.

One study mentioned above concluded that the result of injecting CMA and engaging in unprotected sex "is a perfect storm for transmission of both HIV and hepatitis C as well as a catalogue of ensuing mental health problems." The *Lancet* reports that there is an entire community of IV CMA users in London that is "largely hidden from the gay scene and exists behind closed doors."[2] Intravenous use of CMA in London is "skyrocketing" as is HIV infection. Rehab facilities for gay men seeking treatment for CMA addiction are "overflowing."

In treating a gay man who admits to CMA abuse, we are dealing with a person who is (1) likely HIV positive; (2) has hepatitis C; (3) is somewhat likely to be an intravenous user; (4) is highly likely to have engaged in compulsive sex; and (5) has a very good chance of being a polydrug taker. These other drugs of abuse might include sleeping aids, marijuana, opiates, relaxants, benzodiazepines, antidepressants, and even antipsychotics. We will look at this later.

In addition to the drugs people were taking before they began to use CMA, there is a cocktail of drugs that enhance the actual "experience" of taking CMA or treat problems related to CMA's side effects. Because CMA use can lead to difficulty in maintaining an erection, for example, many of the men reported taking Viagra. To heighten the experience of CMA, some reported using drugs like ketamine (a short-acting dissociative anesthetic that allows one to "check out" their body and "observe" themselves; it is often used as an animal tranquilizer) and/or GHB (gamma hydroxybutyrate, a central nervous system depressant/sedative, also known as the date rape drug).

Most of the men were a 'garbage can' of drug-taking—half of the alphabet!

Indeed, if one cuts to today and goes on a gay dating website, it is not uncommon to see someone advertise "anything goes" and initials like "g, h, v, t, k, or x." These six letters stand for (1) GHB; (2) heroin, (3) Viagra; (4) Tina (another name for CMA); (5) ketamine; and (6) Ecstasy (3, 4-methylenedioxymethamphetamine or MDMA). This combination allows the gay or bisexual man to check out from feelings of guilt and shame, and to heighten the pleasure of forbidden or taboo sexual activity. We will discuss these issues later, but some of the "forbidden or taboo" activities include abusive S&M play, incest and abuse fantasies, "dark" sex, fisting, rape fantasies, orgies, or multiple sexual partners (four or five in one day). Some men on crystal meth can stay in a bathhouse for three or four days in a row without ever eating, leaving, or sleeping. It is easy to understand how a gay or bisexual man would have a tough time disclosing these type of activities in a mixed environment.

This information closely reflects the self-reported drug-taking and sexual habits of many of the men in our study who tried to get clean from CMA. In addition, from my own experience of counseling younger drug users, I would argue that the problem is becoming more acute and is not peaking or ebbing. This intensity of drugs adds to the problem of withdrawal and treatment.

Hence, it is critical to take a holistic view of the gay person's health, a more comprehensive examination than for a relatively healthy person who has a problem with alcohol dependence. This includes helping the gay man learn how to date and regain a healthy perspective on sexual activity, find a spiritual center, take care of health problems, and integrate one's self into the workforce if there has been a period of unemployment.

Indeed, there are very serious psychological, psychiatric, medical, physical, and epidemiological issues that need to be addressed when treating a gay man who is dependent on CMA. (We will also explore this issue in depth in the next chapter.) Many of these men are physically too sick to work. They may be missing teeth—sometimes their front teeth—which makes it difficult to work in a public-facing job. They may have expensive regimens of medication that they cannot afford. Many of them take antidepressants, the effects of which are muted because they often stop taking them when they are "partying." (They also stop taking HIV medications while on "meth runs," and this increases their chances of spreading HIV.) This period of "partying" can last anywhere from twenty-four hours to as long as four of five days. Since they only take these prescribed antidepressants periodically, not only are the mood-stabilizing effects neutralized but their mood swings or depression may actually be aggravated. This makes for mood swings that can be extreme since they are driven by discontinuing antidepressants or mood stabilizers while taking a mix of drugs like CMA, sleeping pills, tranquilizers, and Ecstasy. In the profoundly understated common parlance of the medical community, this combination can have "detrimental social consequences"—such as loss of house, car, job, health, teeth, friends, and personal freedom.

Some of these men have sustained damage in their brains from drug abuse that prevents the natural chemical dopamine from doing its job in the brain's reward system. As a result, the person feels an extended period of flatness, or persistent depression or dysthymia. It is unclear just how long this "flatness" lasts after men stop CMA. It appears that some people bounce back quickly, while many remain in a state of flatness for months, where natural, everyday "up" experiences fail to elevate the person's mood. I worked with one man who said his "flatness" lasted for five years after he stopped taking CMA. The scientific community is still not clear on the long-term consequences of CMA, but some are now claiming that CMA can cause heart attack, cardiomyopathy, seizures, psychosis, and death. We will explore this in chapter 4.

Furthermore, there is a new term referred to as the "second closet." This refers to the way in which HIV-positive men are faced with choices about how and to whom they tell their story and disease status. They fear people finding out at work. They fear family members becoming overly worried about their health if they reveal their status. This leads to poor self-image, depression, loneliness, and romantic detachment.[3] While some HIV-positive men do come to have productive, healthy, and happy lives, many others do not.

THE HIV-NEGATIVE GROUP

Interestingly, the men who went through treatment for dependence on CMA and who were HIV negative had many similar characteristics as the HIV-positive men and were about the same age (they would be about fifty in 2014).

Again, one could infer from their liberal behavior with regard to unprotected passive sex—66 percent reported having unprotected sex and 70 percent reported engaging in compulsive sex—that they were actually on their way to becoming HIV positive.

A significant number of them (15 percent) also reported that they were taking CMA intravenously. We should assume here that, of those who eventually contract HIV, transmission will largely be through unprotected anal sex but also through needle sharing. Both of these behaviors are part of the perfect storm of conditions we referred to earlier that sets someone up for HIV infection. As we have noted, many people who do research on this phenomenon report that the mix of unprotected sex and intravenous CMA use is a potent and dangerous cocktail that often leads to HIV infection.

WERE THE HIV-NEGATIVE MEN AN "HIV ACCIDENT" WAITING TO HAPPEN?

There are two interesting phenomena about this group of gay men who had been treated for CMA dependence. One is that many, 45 percent, reported having a family history of diabetes. This fact merits further attention to determine if causal link exists between drug and alcohol addiction and diabetes. The other phenomenon is also striking: a very high proportion of the gay men who tested HIV negative (as well as those who tested positive) reported a family history of alcoholism. About 80 percent of both of these groups (HIV positive and HIV negative) reported having alcoholism in their families. This, of course, speaks to the genetic element of the disease of addiction. It also speaks to the need for counseling, which can help not only with relapse prevention but also with family-of-origin childhood trauma. Both of these are necessary, in my opinion, for effective relapse prevention.

The body of statistical data that has coalesced in the past few years suggests that many of these HIV-negative men were a case of HIV "waiting to happen." It is impossible to know what happened to them since the study, but I would wager that more than half of them are, by now, HIV positive. After all, one in six was already using CMA intravenously and two out of three were practicing unsafe sex. One would hope for an outcome of continued "sobriety" from CMA, but the numbers do not offer a high degree of confidence that these men were ultimately able to stay "clean and sober" on a long-term basis.

Many in the heterosexual community blithely say, "Why don't these guys just stop partying and having unsafe sex?" Indeed, the behavior of young gay men in their twenties is especially vexing to some, since this group has grown up in an increasingly accepting and gay-friendly environment. Though they may not face the same sort of societal stigma that their predecessors endured, the numbers of gay and bisexual homeless are still disturbingly high—as are the numbers of men in their twenties who are contracting HIV. And the numbers of men who are using hard drugs like CMA is at record levels in cities such as London. Part of this phenomenon can be attributed to "HIV fatigue."[4] That is, many gay and bisexual men ruminate what life would be like if they contracted HIV. They know that every single act of sexually acting out may be life-changing and poses a potential challenge to their mental and physical well-being. This threat produces homo-negativity and other negative effects, such as depression and anxiety. These negative feelings, in turn, could lead to alcohol and drug dependence. Furthermore, some gay men arrive at a point where they essentially say, "Let's just get this over with." No longer wishing to be burdened by the anxiety of becoming HIV, they decide to do their best to contract it; they let themselves be "bred." They may rationalize this decision, saying that HIV is only a chronic condition, controllable with medications, and no longer a death sentence. So, they think, living with HIV may not be that bad.

This is not, of course, an ideal outcome and there is controversy in the gay community about how hard to come down on this attitude. Some want to communicate a more unequivocal message to avoid any sexual activity that could lead to HIV infection. Others are of the mind that people should be free to make their own decisions and that the issue of HIV should not be turned into a "badge of shame." Therefore, aggressively attacking the means by which HIV is contracted can be seen as politically controversial. This issue needs far deeper dialogue.

The proliferation of drug and alcohol dependence in the new generation of gay and bisexual men who have had a more gay-friendly adolescence is mysterious. Recall the previously mentioned study that shows an all-time high number of men seeking rehab in London. My own experience working with drug and alcohol facilities in Asia suggests that more and more young people are experiencing CMA dependence in this region of the world as well. In particular, within the past two years or so, CMA has been moving into the gay scene at a rapid pace. Many Asian cities are not ready for what is about to hit. China is making vast quantities of CMA. In December 2013, a raid in a village in Guangdong uncovered three tonnes of finished CMA and twenty-three tonnes of chemical raw materials. The problems will certainly grow in places like greater China before it shrinks.

THE DEAD

Now we get to the group that is perhaps the most intriguing—those who cannot speak for themselves because they are dead. Nine men died between the time this group began to receive treatment for CMA dependence and the time the study was initiated. This was over a period of about five years. From the data, here is how and why they died: These men were born, on average, in 1963 and did everything early. They would have been about forty-one or forty-two when they died in about 2002 or 2003. Their death certificates listed a wide range of causes of death. A few died of "diabetes mellitus," a few from "heart attack," but none of "accidental drug overdose." Isn't it remarkable that death certificates so seldom reveal that a "drug overdose" or "acute alcoholism" was the cause of death? Alcoholism has been classified as a disease just like diabetes or cancer, and yet it is so rarely cited as an official cause of death on these documents.

THE DEAD: IV USE, CRIMINALITY, UNSAFE SEX, PROSTITUTION AND MOST HAD BI-POLAR

These men began experimenting with alcohol and drugs, on average, at age of thirteen, and most came from families that had alcoholism. They dropped out of school early as well or barely finished high school. Furthermore, they were ahead of their peers in their contraction of HIV, which most acquired at about age twenty-five. This would have been about 1988, a time when the drug cocktails for treating HIV were not yet advanced. Most of these men were intravenous drugs users, were poly-drug users, and were smokers. They had a high prevalence of hepatitis, and their levels of diabetes were also very high. When it comes to sexual acting out, most reported they were compulsive. All of them reported that they engaged in unsafe sex. Almost half of them had legal troubles. Several reported that they engaged in "pay for play."

The dead men had a very different drug history from that of the HIV-positive living men. They all began using drugs and alcohol in their early teens and their drugs of choice tended to be heavier drugs such as LSD, heroin, and cocaine. This speaks to the need to implement more realistic and focused drug prevention programs for high-risk twelve- to fourteen-year-olds—not waiting until they are fifteen to seventeen years old, when it may be too late. There is also a need to address early signs of mental illness on a realistic and forceful manner for at-risk teens in the twelve-to-fourteen age range, since many of the signs of what are now easily treated illnesses can be detected at this age. One study, for instance, indicated that adolescent bipolar disorder can be detected as early as age five or six. It is never too soon to discuss these topics with young people. Further, it is wise for adolescents to have an honest discussion around the dinner table with their parents about their family history of mental disorders. We will see in a moment while this type of discussion is so relevant to this death study. In addition, multiple studies have concluded that adolescents with these types of disorders have a substantially higher chance of developing problems with alcohol and drug abuse.[5]

THE DEAD WERE INTO HARD DRUGS BY HIGH SCHOOL

If we compare the history of drug-taking between the living and the dead, 62 percent of the HIV-infected living men used only alcohol and marijuana before embarking on CMA use. (They began to use heavier drugs such as Ecstasy, ketamine, and GHB only *after* their meth use began.) This is an important clue to CMA prevention. Many people who tried CMA for the first time were not typical drug takers but instead casual pot smokers or people who drank alcohol "frequently." These are run-of-the-mill gay men who went to clubs to have a good time, and in these or other social settings they were introduced to CMA. Many of these men say they began to use CMA "casually" in a club in order to "get more energy" or "to dance longer." However, the casual first use eventually led to long-term catastrophic consequences. This pattern reveals why it is important to communicate the dangers of CMA use not to a specific group of 'high risk' drug users but to the larger community as a whole. Even people who rarely use alcohol or others drug—and those with university degrees and successful careers—are often just as likely to fall into the CMA trap as those with a clear history of drug and alcohol abuse from an early age.

Another difference between the living and the dead was that 55 percent of the dead men were IV users versus 15 percent of the HIV-negative men. It appears that these men started using hard-core drugs in a hard-core way at a young age and very quickly were faced with a host of seemingly intractable problems. The collection of problems includes hepatitis C from IV use, HIV from IV use and/or unprotected sex, criminal prosecution, smoking, derailed educational development, broken relationships, family alienation, and presumed self-loathing from being gay. The runaway train began at twelve or thirteen and was seemingly unstoppable. Or was it?

The statistics to back up these claims are as follows:

- 80 percent of the dead men smoked cigarettes versus 33 percent of the HIV-infected living men.
- 44 percent of the dead men had felony convictions versus 4 percent of the HIV-infected living men.
- The mean level of education of the dead was twelfth grade versus two years of college for the HIV-infected living men.

- By the age of seventeen, these men would have fallen out of the typical system of education and adult development. Incarceration, rehabs, halfway houses, probation officers, and drug addiction itself would have derailed their lives by the time they were 20 years old.

MOST OF THE DEAD HAD BIPOLAR DISORDER

Perhaps the most noteworthy discovery was the very high number of men with bipolar disorder among the dead. Five of these nine men had bipolar versus 8 percent of the HIV-infected living men.[6] They had been taking bipolar medications off and on for many years, including lithium. The issue of co-occurring disorders is currently getting more attention than ever and the interest is only growing. Many leaders in the Twelve Step movement now recommend that psychiatric and psychological issues be addressed in conjunction with a social and spiritual course of Twelve Step work. There is a greater sense of acceptance among adults when it comes to access and understanding the vast array of disorders. And there is a movement afoot by doctors to demystify this list of disorders (as identified in the American Psychiatric Associations' *Diagnostic and Statistical Manual of Mental Disorders* [DSM]) and make it accessible to a larger audience and to remove the stigma attached to mental illness. Lastly, society as a whole (at least in the West) is more comfortable with a public discussion of mental illness in a way that is compassionate and familiar. In many parts of Asia, however, much work still needs to be done to demystify mental disorders for the general public.

One of the well-known writers on bipolar disorder is Kay Redfield Jamison. On the connection between addiction and bipolar disorder, she commented, when depression or bipolar disorder is accompanied by alcohol or drug abuse, the risk of suicide increases perilously. This is because people with addiction and bipolar disorder often end up in a state of cold, agitated despair. . . . The burden [they] know themselves to be to others is intolerable."[7] Isolation breeds further isolation. Mental illness compounds. These men were likely escaping the voices and the depression when they were twelve or thirteen by using drugs and no one was around to offer a diagnosis to their mental illness. In this way, we may be able to see alcohol and drugs as a self-diagnosis by the person to escape the mania, the depression, and the mad feelings.

The gay community has come very far in this regard as well. Today we have much success with integrating medical regimens not only for HIV but also for mental health disorders into a holistic discussion of social and spiritual development. A thorny issue for the Twelve Step community to resolve centers around the spiritual aspect of the program, since many gay men have a sour taste in their mouths from previous experiences with religions that have been, to say the least, unwelcome to gay people.

As we will discuss later in this book, some gay men often have no faith in some higher power (or even in themselves?) because they have been asked to leave faith communities. They have no heroes because there are few openly gay members of the community. Furthermore, too much of gay community life revolves around bars, clubs, and other forms of entertainment that involve alcohol and drugs. One metastudy of gay, lesbian, and bisexual people suggested that GLB people are two times more likely than heterosexuals to develop problems with alcohol or substance abuse. In addition, bisexual youth are three and a half more likely than heterosexual youth to develop problems with drug and alcohol abuse. It seems that bisexual youth have an even more difficult time than gay people.[8]

If we delve further into the actual behavior that differentiates the dead from the living, we glimpse a more accurate and darker picture. Of the dead men, 88 percent reported having had suicidal thoughts versus 46 percent of the living HIV-infected men and 37 percent of the living HIV-negative men. Fewer of the dead men were taking antidepressants (66 percent) than the living HIV-infected men (88 percent). We can speculate that either they could not afford these medications, they stopped taking them during drug-taking activity, or they were never diagnosed. What we know for sure is that the dead men represented more than a third of all the self-reported bipolar men in the entire study.

This is the debate (and the dilemma) of co-occurring disorders. Did bipolar disorder kill these men? Did they have one too many manic phases or deep depressions that they tried to pull out of with excessive drug use? Did they use drugs or alcohol to drown out the "voices" or the "chattering committee"? Or did bipolar play only a minor role in stoking the other world of drug dependence? The recent metastudies discussed in this chapter indicate that co-occurring disorders such as anxiety, bipolar, and ADHD may actually precede the onset of alcohol and drug abuse. Nonetheless, it is increasingly common in the treatment community to treat co-occurring disorders in tandem with drug and alcohol abuse. Treatments for drug addiction alone, without addressing other disorders, may be a waste of money and a dead end.

Are we kidding ourselves to think we can so easily separate out in neat categories the "drug-related" cause of death versus the "bipolar" cause of death? The death certificates of these men do not say they died of either "acute alcoholism" or "adult-onset bipolar disorder." If we rely on the stated cause of death, we would conclude that virtually no one dies from alcoholism or from bipolar disorder outcomes such as suicide. They die from something else—they slip and die from injuries sustained in a fall; they have a fatal brain aneurism; the cause of death is related to their diabetes. The men in the study did not die from bipolar disorder either, but the numbers are too high to conclude that bipolar behavior had nothing to do with their deaths. Still, it is hard to know what really happened, and the true cause of death is a mystery. Therein lies the deep difficulty of co-occurring disorders. Since it is unclear how people actually die of this disease, it is hard to know how to prevent death. Much of this has to do with the social stigmas that are still attached to alcoholism and mental disorders. It seems no one wants to poison the family line by claiming such a disease on a death certificate.

Again, we can pick up the thread from an earlier chapter from Kay Redfield Jamison who said that addiction mixed with bipolar disorder is a perilous combination and can explain more than a few suicides. Too often, she continues, physicians pitch their tent in a psycho-pharmaceutical camp like the psychiatrist who prescribed Roger a host of medications without taking into account the difference between symptoms of mental illness and symptoms of withdrawal from drugs. Or, they pitch their tent in the psychotherapy camp and insist that logotherapy can deal with the problem. Redfield Jamison insists both are important. Empathy and competence with both drugs and therapy is the way out.[9]

Unfortunately, many more questions than answers arise when we uncover a more complete picture of these men. What could have been done to prevent their deaths or steer them from the rocky shores of CMA? It seems that any kind of intervention or attempt to slow down or arrest their drug intake would be secondary to the deeper issues of bipolar disorder. The ideal intervention would have been an aggressive educational campaign during junior high to highlight the dangers of using drugs along with a sober and straightforward discussion of warning signs of various disorders that may arise in late adolescence. Discussions led by teachers and parents about these signs—and a candid discussion about family history of psychological disorders—would be appropriate.

On the one hand, the dark moods of depression, suicidal ideation, isolation, and self-loathing could lead such a person to seek out any means to escape from morbid thoughts or depressive moods, to gratefully use any drug that would ward off feelings of helplessness, impotence, self-despair, and suicidality. And since the high from CMA can produce feelings of being invincible, highly sexualized, and super confident, using CMA makes sense to a person confined in the dark despair that occurs during the depressive phase of a bipolar cycle. Using this drug also makes a special kind of sense for a gay person who has an identity that is partially formed. They are not in the mainstream of heterosexual life but not yet fully formed and self-loving gay men. They are lost in a world of half-truths, lies, and deception. They are "spies" in the midst of an enemy afraid of the consequences of being "caught."

On the other hand, manic moods, which can lead to erratic behavior, flights of fancy, or phenomenal boosts of energy that keep the person up for days, feel wonderful to the person with bipolar disorder. When these moods begin to wear off, would it not make sense to try CMA in order to keep the "high"? I have heard this rationale many times from individuals in treatment. Indeed, taking CMA to extend the manic phase and to curtail the depressive phase is logical to a CMA addict.

This leads us to the same question that is often found in recent literature: Is it desirable or even possible to intervene and treat addiction before some form of medical history is gleaned from the addict? Along those same lines, is it possible that those who died due to complications from drug and alcohol abuse could have been saved had they been treated for co-occurring disorders? Many of the men who died were at one point diagnosed with some kind of co-occurring disorder and had a history of taking lithium. They either self-reported they were diagnosed and/or they self-reported they were taking lithium; this was part of the medical history. Even so, could we realistically expect rehab centers, charged with helping hundreds of men under the influence of CMA and other drugs to get clean and begin building lives in recovery, to somehow force these addicts to follow their doctor's recommendations for taking appropriate medications for co-occurring disorders?

Indeed, this is a common struggle for gay and straight addicts and alcoholics who have a co-occurring mental health disorder. Many of these people have been prescribed various medications for anxiety, depression, psychosis, and so forth. During drug-taking episodes, addicts often report that they forget to take their medications. As a result, the other symptoms we have mentioned rise to the surface and more drugs and/or alcohol are required to alter or repress the disturbing feelings—feelings that the drugs prescribed by the psychiatrist were intended to address.

In short, the person used illegal drugs—CMA, cocaine, crack, or heroin, for example—to mask the symptoms that legal prescription medications were intended to address. In the eyes of the addict, the dealer becomes a substitute for the doctor. The addict abuses the prescription medications by forgetting to take them and instead turns to another type of drug abuse (mostly the illegal type) to quell or suppress feelings of depression, apartness, psychosis, paranoia, or even suicidality that accompany a legitimate mental illness.

A nationally acclaimed doctor with whom I worked with on this study was disturbed by what we found. Of the cluster of men who died, the majority had bipolar disorder. He said, "Untreated bipolar disorder is a real killer—maybe more of a killer than drugs and alcohol." He shook his head in sadness and spoke of the difficulty in trying to treat a person's addiction to CMA when there is a kaleidoscope of problems lurking in the background. These problems include (1) a higher-than-average incidence of alcoholism among gay people; (2) profoundly low self-esteem stemming from societal messages that gay people are somehow bad or evil; (3) higher-than-average levels of depression among gay people; and (4) higher-than-average incidence of bipolar disorder in gay men.

In the past few years, we have witnessed many advances in the treatment of bipolar disorder. Hundreds of thousands of people with this disorder now lead perfectly normal lives. The wonderful autobiography of Kay Redfield Jamison called *An Unquiet Mind* is a fascinating exploration of someone learning how to live with bipolar disorder. Yet in the area of addiction—and particularly in the area of gay men in addiction—there is still much to learn about the interaction between addiction and co-occurring disorders such as bipolar and issues involving depression, anxiety, alienation, and antisocial behavior.

One of the reasons that the study discussed in this chapter was not published was because the doctors involved were justifiably uncomfortable with the results. These were experts in the field of CMA, not experts on psychiatric disorders like bipolar disorder. The study of CMA addiction is a very narrow and focused slice of the medical community and including co-occurring disorders can cause CMA specialists justifiable discomfort as they are veer away from their established specialty and invite criticism from specialists in bipolar disorder. Further, this was only one study. If we provided compelling evidence that bipolar disorder was responsible for most of the deaths in this group of gay men who were seeking treatment, is it possible that another study would reveal the same results? It is likely but cannot be proven. Furthermore, this was a fairly small sample of only 110 gay men.

So, the study was simply set aside. The reason that I discuss it now is that, since the study, I have encountered many individual cases of people who are trying to get clean from alcohol and drugs (including many gay men) and who have been diagnosed with co-occurring disorders but who do nothing about these disorders while they try to get clean and sober. The result is chronic relapse. My own experience is that the chances of sustained recovery are improved greatly when people take prescribed medications for mental disorders while following a regimen for drug and alcohol treatment. This includes support from a network of family and friends, therapy, and/or some form of Twelve Step work.

ROGER'S STORY

I once worked with a crystal meth addict who was taking CMA intravenously. A Latino man, Roger was twenty-eight when we met and had been using CMA for several years. He had begun to take CMA intravenously when he was twenty-five. Roger was only fifteen when he began acting out sexually—visiting truck stops near his hometown and having anonymous sex with truck drivers. All the time that he was living at home, he felt ashamed of his sexuality and kept this part of his life a secret from his family. He tested HIV positive when he was twenty-five, but likely had contracted the virus long before then, he said. Although he had been prescribed medications for bipolar disorder when he was in his early twenties, he had stopped taking them, he said, because they made him feel as if he were "living outside his body."

When I met Roger, he was trying to get clean and sober in a rehab in Los Angeles. He was in his first week of treatment when we met, and he was still visibly agitated and often irrational from the aftereffects of CMA. At the end of his first week, he visited a psychiatrist and returned with five different medications. These were medications to help with anxiety, psychosis, paranoia, depression, and sleeplessness, all of which he reported experiencing. I am sure the psychiatrist he saw knew that Roger was in recovery from CMA addiction. Roger seemed to be quite knowledgeable about all of them and was conversant in the "lingo" of which drugs go with which symptom of drug withdrawal. This was not his first time getting batches of medications.

When I saw this cornucopia of drugs, I wondered if the mixture of benzodiazepines and other drugs was going to be effective at all. Here is a case of someone who appeared to be sincere about stopping CMA (intravenously) and was also claiming to have psychosis, paranoia, sleeplessness, anxiety, and severe depression. Every one of the medications prescribed by the psychiatrist may have been appropriate for a "normal" person who was exhibiting these individual symptoms. However, it seems a real stretch to say that it was appropriate for a CMA addict with these symptoms to be prescribed a separate drug for each symptom. After all, the common signs of withdrawal from CMA are the very symptoms named above—paranoia, psychosis, sleeplessness, anxiety, and depression.

Is this just bad medicine? Or is the rehab community failing to have a sincere dialogue with the psychiatric community? I will discuss the latter question in a bit. When it comes to the former question, most of these drugs are themselves addictive. And the cocktail of drugs would, at the very least, cause feelings of being "checked out."

Roger's case is an extreme one, but it shows the kind of overkill that can result when a doctor gives separate medications for each (and expected or normal!) sign of withdrawal from CMA. Many people recovering from CMA end up in low-cost rehab centers (or jail) and have no access to medications that would help them "come down" from the multifarious mood swings, paranoia, psychosis, and depression that are common in withdrawal. People who enter Twelve Step programs such as Crystal Meth Anonymous also may not have any access to medications that would help relieve with these symptoms. In fact, some uninformed people in Twelve Step programs actively discourage the use of any type of medication in the recovery process—arguing that sobriety is "being free of any drugs from the neck up." Clearly, this is going to the other end extreme and can lead to another set of severe problems. In addition, this kind of forceful advice is completely at odds with the philosophy of the foundations of Alcoholics Anonymous, which states that "we know only a little."

Is Roger's case one of replacing illegal stimulants with legalized opiates or benzodiazepines, which can lead to their own kinds of addiction, abuse, and poor outcomes? I say that the answer to this question is a guarded yes. Is it a case of the community of drug counselors failing to have any real kind of discussion with the community of doctors who prescribe medications? Absolutely! Many medical doctors spend little time understanding alternative programs for recovery. Is it a case of doctors who have little confidence in the spiritual or psychological elements of recovery? Yes. Should doctors offer prescriptions for certain types of moods when they know these moods are a result of illegal substance abuse? The answers here are unclear. How is a person supposed to make behavioral changes, reflect on his history of drug abuse, work to mend relationships with family and friends, and complete other recovery-related tasks with this pharmaceutical alphabet soup swirling around his head? Roger was just plain strung out and suffering from CMA withdrawal. In many ways, taking these meds was worse than just enduring the withdrawal from CMA. Furthermore, is a person who is a newly sober drug addict and who has self-reported depression really going to take the correct dose of antidepressants? Will a person with self-reported delusionality and paranoia take the correct dose of antipsychotic medications? Will a person with self-reported high levels of anxiety take the correct dose of antianxiety medications, which are benzodiazepines and which are themselves highly addictive? The answers are somewhat self-evident. No, this is all unlikely.

In layman's terms, giving a drug addict who is a CMA user (who is in his first week of recovery) a cornucopia of antipsychotics, anxiety reducers, antidepressants, and sleep aids is a recipe for disaster. The person will most likely abuse the drugs from the doctor and then return to CMA use. And this

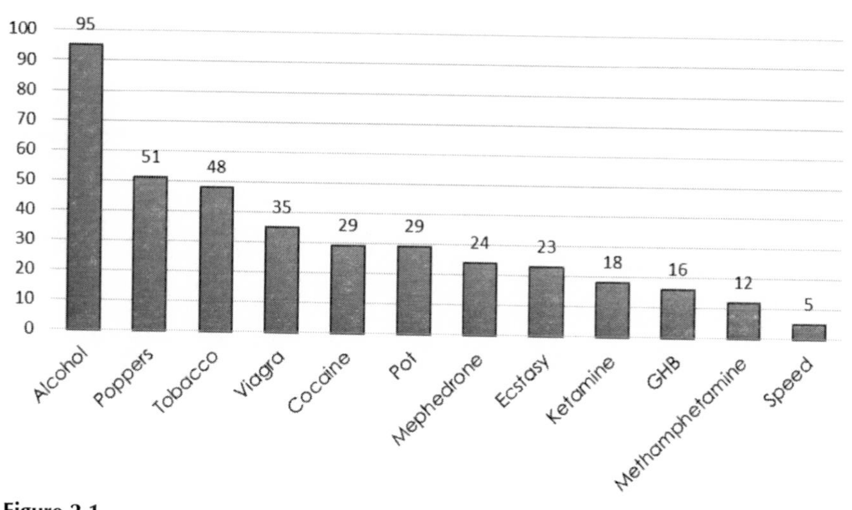

Figure 2.1.
Source: 2014 Chemsex Study: London School of Hygiene and Tropical Medicine

is precisely what happened to Roger. When he finished the prescribed medications, he returned to intravenous CMA use. When I last heard from him, he was using CMA somewhere in central California. The person who managed the rehab facility Roger attended had appropriately allowed him to visit his psychiatrist and to bring prescribed medications into the rehab—all five of them. The problem was that the manager of the facility knew virtually nothing about the individual drugs and was simply following orders.

So, on the one hand, we have psychiatrists who are willing to prescribe any number of medications (most of which are addictive) to addicts who are coming down from drugs such as CMA. On the other hand, there are Twelve Step fanatics who insist that any kind of "drug" use (SSRI antidepressants, bipolar disorder medications, etc.) is clear evidence that the person is not sober. Surely we can find a middle ground. On this score, UCLA has tried a number of drugs to help users of CMA to "come down" from the dangerous effects of the drug. Dr. Steve Shoptaw is the lead scientist on many of these studies. He has initiated studies using certain SSRIs and another drug called Promote. The results are mixed.

The difference being discussed here is a vital one. There is the reality of drug addiction and withdrawal from addiction. And there are psychological and psychiatric issues which arise in the process of detoxing from an array of drugs. Too many doctors seem to be addressing the former and not the latter. Indeed, the DSM makes a distinction between mood disorders which are present in recovery and which have been present for a considerable period of time AND those disorders such as mood, anxiety, or dementia disorders which

LONDON CHEMSEX STUDY: METEORIC RISE IN "SLAMMING" OF CMA AND MEPHEDRONE

Adam Bourne and his colleagues at the London School of Hygiene & Tropical Medicine have published an excellent study on substance abuse and sexual activity in London.[1] This was published in 2014, concentrates on a heavily gay area of London (Lambeth, Southwark, and Lewisham) and included men with a mean age of thirty-eight. Its conclusions match and exceed the hoary conclusions of the study in Los Angeles. The conclusions will match the tone of this book which is that, despite greater openness and acceptance of gay life in society, the level of self-destructive behavior in the gay community seems to be intensifying. Greater openness toward gay and bisexual men and lesbians should lead to reduced stress, greater job opportunities, less discrimination and bullying and less stigmatization. And yet . . . Here are some of the conclusions reached in a survey that included more than 1,000 participants:

1. In 2005, only 3 percent of the gay and bisexual population self-reported that they had tried crystal meth, GHB, and mephedrone. By 2012, it was 85 percent. Nearly all crystal meth use was reported in sexual settings.
2. One clinic reported that one in five had recently used GHB and one in 10 had used crystal meth. 80 percent of men who had reported using crystal meth said they had used it intravenously. Other clinics reported that of their clients were using crystal meth, almost half were injecting crystal meth.
3. Crystal meth causes high-risk sexual behaviors, especially in poly drug environments which include GHB, crystal meth, Viagra, Ecstasy, and cocaine.
4. These gay men have even coined a phrase for GHB overdoses given their commonality. It is called "G sleep" and includes unconsciousness, choking, and respiratory depression.
5. One in five men are living with HIV in this borough, versus 14 percent in greater London. The numbers vary widely but the increase in those who slam CMA has risen from 1percent in 2001 to more than half by 2012.
6. The study asked what percent had consumed a drug in the past six months: alcohol (95 percent); tobacco (48 percent); amyl nitrate (51percent); Viagra (35 percent); Ecstasy (23 percent) crystal meth (12 percent); mephadrone (24 percent); GHB (16 percent); cocaine (29 percent). These shocking data speak to a community which is lost in addiction and needs a great deal of compassion and understanding given destroyed health, careers, friendships, and self-esteem.

7. The report suggests clear, honest, and non-judgmental information about how to use drugs and have chemsex safely. Is this enough? I think there is a groundswell of opinion which says that more frank, open, candid, and forceful language is required. After all, according to the National HIV Surveillance System, 60 percent of new HIV cases are from gay and bisexual men. If this alarming spread is not arrested, gay communities in urban areas globally risk devolving into an irreversible health crisis.

Note

1. A. Bourne, D. Reid, F. Hickson, Rueda S. Torres, P. Weatherburn (2014) The Chemsex study: Drug use in sexual settings among gay & bisexual men in Lambeth, Southwark & Lewisham. London: Sigma Research, London School of Hygiene & Tropical Medicine.

are induced by drugs and alcohol and which may be present in someone like Roger who still has drugs in his bloodstream. Unfortunately, the results from the coverage of the medical records and self-reported drug taking of most of these gay men who were in treatment for CMA includes a cornucopia of pharmaceuticals which covers benzos, stimulants, sleeping aids, antipsychotics, and antidepressants.

Table 2.1 shows three different types of withdrawal symptoms: delusionality, dementia, and mood disorders. One is a skewed emotional response to the world. One indicates impaired brain function. And the others indicate behaviors which veer far from the normal. Roger was one week in a rehab and was given an array of medications because he could not sleep, think, emote, or act in a normal fashion. Does anyone who is a week clean from slamming CMA on a regular basis exhibit anything but the symptoms below? The same goes for severe abuse of crack, cocaine or, for that matter, severe abuse of alcohol. Perhaps greater care is required in order to ensure that a passage of

Table 2.1.

Common side-effects from drugs in Day 1 to 60.
Substance-induced Delirium
Substance-induced Persisting Dementia
Substance-induced Amnesiac Disorder
Substance-induced Psychotic Disorder
Substance-induced Mood Disorder
Substance-induced Anxiety Disorder
Substance-induced Sexual Dysfunction
Substance-induced Sleep Disorder

time (about 30 days) before a panoply of drugs is thrown at a newly clean or sober individual.

The last time I heard from Roger, he called me from central California and was just about to slam more CMA. He said, "I can't believe I am doing this after everything I know!" I never heard from him again.

Furthermore, we can look at Table 2.2 and see the short-term and long-term signs of withdrawal from various families of drugs. One of the controversial issues among the second category (cocaine and CMA) is the extent to which longer-term withdrawal symptoms can morph into disorders such as major depression. CMA offers a sense of power and strength, as well as sexual prowess, in a world that has often treated this gay man as a marginal or even undesirable part of society. He is often ashamed of his own sexual desires and CMA allows this shame to disappear. The addictive hook on CMA is understandable, but the long-term withdrawal symptoms causes this gay man to pay a very high price for the desire to escape society, remove himself from his own shame and low self-esteem in a kind of out-of-body experience and have mind-blowing sex. However, there is a plethora of research on the short and medium term damage to the brain from CMA, but my own experience is that men in recovery for CMA abuse can exhibit something like major depression for a year or more after stopping. Most textbooks say that people in recovery from drug and alcohol dependence should not receive any diagnosis of disorders in the first 30 or even 60 days of recovery. The issue is that in the case of CMA, the damage to the body could cause withdrawal symptoms such as depression, dysthymia, paranoia, or psychosis which could last for several months. Herein lies the problem with gay man and crystal meth. How much damage has been done, how much of it is irreversible and is there a generally agreed upon timeline for the dissipation of these symptoms? Researchers are honing in quickly on these questions, but there does not yet seem to be a consensus on any of these difficult questions.

Many in the community ask themselves what kind of treatments are appropriate for men who have been clean from CMA for three or six months and still feel severe depression or anhedonia. Even those who adhere to weekly therapy and regular meetings of CMA or AA can report feeling low and depressed, although feelings of suicidality do diminish. In this way, stopping is much better than starting. But the neural network of a man who has taken CMA for a considerable period of time is not fully recovered to deliver the endorphins to reinforce a "job well done" for staying clean. Many of these men take antidepressants without a great deal of success. In addition, sex is just not what it used to be, so there is a flat-lining when it comes to sexual intimacy. Consequently, it is possible to have a man in recovery who is six

Table 2.2.

NO DIAGNOSIS SHOULD EVER BE MADE DURING DETOXIFICATION/WITHDRAWAL.				
DRUG	*EFFECT*	*DEPENDENCE*	*ACUTE WITHDRAWAL*	*LONGER TERM WITHDRAWAL (6–12 MTS)*
Alcohol	EUPHORIA, CONFIDENCE	VIOLENCE, LOWERED IMPULSE CONTROL	ANXIETY, DTs, INSOMNIA, DEATH	FATIGUE, INSTABILITY, HOSTILITY
Crystal meth	**POWER, STRENGTH, LIBODO**	**IMPULSIVE, DANGEROUS BEHAVIOR**	**FATIGUE, SUICIDALITY, DEPRESSION, PARANOIA**	**ANHEDONIA, MAJOR DEPRESSION, DYSTHYMIA, SUICIDALITY, PSYCHOSIS**
Hallucinogens	DETACH FROM SELF	PANIC, PARANOIA	PSYCHOSIS	FLASHBACKS
Opioids	INTENSE EUPHORIA	STOPPING CREATES NEED FOR MORE	ACUTE ANXIETY AGITATION	ANXIETY, DEPRESSION, INSOMNIA
Sedatives	EUPHORIA, CONFIDENCE	NO IMPULSE CONTROL, OFTEN VIOLENCE	ANXIETY, INSOMNIA, NAUSEA, DEATH	ANXIETY, DEPRESSION, EAR RINGING

months or even one year clean from CMA but who is depressed and incapable of any intimacy.

There is nothing else to say about this except that the road to permanent sobriety from CMA is hard and very painful. Some men report that normal feelings of enjoyment, peace of mind, and balance return after six months to one year. Some men report that normality in sexual behavior can take one to two years. I think it takes one year for a gay man who has abused CMA for a considerable period of time to gain an even keel and begin to feel more normal with regard to thinking, feeling, acting, and behaving. The community does not need to deceive itself about the pain required and the length of time required to feel better after long periods of abuse with CMA. This reality must be discussed far more publicly. Hiding from or skirting the difficulty of recovery will only add to the relapse rate as gay men in recovery from CMA abuse think that they are too sick to hear the truth.

In conclusion, what subsequently happened to the living members of the death study? How many more died? Did some finally "get it" and achieve long-term sobriety? Did the ones who were HIV negative remain negative? The current data suggests that these gay men likely did not fare well. For example, a 2013 *Lancet* study found that (a) CMA use is clearly on the rise in London (and cases of HIV are on the rise in Los Angeles, New York City, Sydney, Singapore, San Francisco, and Hong Kong (where cases of HIV transmission hit a new high in Q1 2014); (b) drug treatment clinics, particularly in London, are massively overcrowded and struggling to cope; and (c) Asia is being hit with a proliferation of CMA only in the past two years, so the governments there need to be prepared for significant consequences for the gay and bisexual working population, i.e., absenteeism, sickness, hospital visits, overdoses, and long term treatment facilities.

In London in 2011, there was a record 3,010 HIV cases of men who have sex with men.[10] Injection of CMA is also on the rise. Recall that 66 percent of the men in the study laid out earlier who tested HIV negative admitted they were not practicing safe sex. Further, 15 percent of these men were also using CMA intravenously. So, we should assume that many of them also contracted HIV within the past few years. These men who bottom without using condoms or who use CMA through an IV method (often shared) are prime candidates for HIV infection. For them, it is almost a given that they will become HIV positive. In fact, by the time most men enter their second rehab, they have a 50 percent chance of being HIV positive. By the time they enter a rehab for the third time, their chances of being HIV positive are 90 percent.[11]

In conclusion, we see that even into the teen years of this century, more and more gay men are drawn to dangerous drugs like crystal meth and are more likely to engage in risky sexual activity when on this drug. This often leads to

MICHAEL'S STORY

Michael is a twenty-nine-year-old American male who went to the best prep schools in the country and to an Ivy League university. Behind this façade of success, however, was a wounded youth who would learn as a teenager that his biological father committed suicide when Michael was a young boy. From an early age, he was finishing the drinks that grown-ups had abandoned at parties. He was sent to an elite boarding school at the age of nine, and he began using alcohol and drugs at thirteen. By the time he entered college, Michael was doing Ecstasy and LSD. By twenty, he was getting high on meth and was snorting heroin to come back down. He managed to clean himself up for a few years, but by the age of twenty-four was back on meth, alcohol, and cocaine.

At age twenty-seven, he left a committed relationship and started leading a promiscuous lifestyle. His business failed and his meth habit accelerated. He could go for days (sometimes seven or eight days) without sleep, but this eventually led to hallucinations, raging blackouts, paranoia, and, as he put it, "twisted sex." His bottom occurred while standing on the top of a building in Los Angeles contemplating suicide.

He sought help and checked into the Betty Ford Clinic where he was strongly urged to stay for three months. He was defeated enough to agree and actively participated in all of the programs the rehab offered. The cognitive behavioral therapy and the written "life timeline" were particularly helpful to him. Reflecting on his past and on how he had arrived at the point of desperation was illuminating, indeed. The therapist's approach to discussing childhood trauma was very helpful. And sleep—lots of sleep. The center allowed him to sleep as much as seventeen hours a day for the first week.

After he left the Betty Ford Center, he immediately jumped into Twelve Step meetings, attending fifteen per week. He was very active in service work. He also cut off all communication with his drug-addled past, erasing all phone numbers and avoiding the places where he formerly hung out. His attitude was, "Do this or you are dead."

After a few months, he began to experience periods of joy as well as occasional times of flatness. Michael now practices a spiritual program of morning meditation. Three years into his recovery, he still attends regular Twelve Step meetings, has a good job, and maintains a clear mind. He has a partner and is in a loving relationship. He has been able to stay sober, he says, by using the skills he learned at Betty Ford, by working a rigorous and disciplined Twelve Step program, and relying on the fellowship and support it offers.

HIV infection. Recent literature noted in this book shows an out-of-control situation in most gay meccas, London in particular. There is even a subculture in London that has elaborate secret parties at which dozens of people get together to use CMA intravenously. Self-loathing behavior, HIV fatigue, low self-esteem, and drug abuse lead to a potent cocktail of HIV, unemployment, chronic health issues, destroyed relationships, and wrecked careers. This exacts a high cost from society and needs much more attention, especially in cities around the world where CMA is a new and rising phenomenon. These cities include Tokyo, Hong Kong, and Singapore. Asia is now facing an onslaught of CMA abuse, particularly in Hong Kong and Singapore. The anecdotal evidence in Hong Kong and Singapore is disturbing and there clearly needs to be a wake-up call for police, medical, hospital, and clinic staffs to create a coordinated effort for prevention, intervention, and treatment of this scourge. See Appendix 1 which describes the chronology of the drug use of the living and the dead men.

SIMILARITIES AND DIFFERENCES BETWEEN THE DEAD AND THE LIVING

There were many differences between the lifestyles and choices of the living and the dead. The dead were drinking alcohol, smoking pot, taking drugs at a much earlier age of around thirteen. They were using CMA by the age of twenty-one or twenty-two or so, which set them up for many negative consequences in by their mid 20s. One of these consequences is that they were 5 times more likely to have some criminal conviction. They were 3 times more likely to smoke. They were far more likely to have contracted Hepatitis C, most likely from injecting CMA. Their college careers would have gone up in smoke. They would have contracted HIV by about twenty-five. Most important, however, is that they had a far higher propensity to show signs of bipolar behavior and were intermittently self-reporting that they were taking bipolar medications.

There were some interesting similarities between the living and the dead. Both had high levels of Hepatitis C. About 80 percent of both groups reported that they had alcoholism in their family histories. Both groups reported very high levels of diabetes. Both groups had a lapse of ten years between the first drink and first meth use. This may be an accidental outcome.

Summary of Recommendations (1) Programs for alcohol and drug treatment, education, and interdiction should move into the twelve-to-fourteen age group. (2) The dangers of CMA should be given paramount attention. (3) Children should be actively encouraged to discuss the history of alcoholism in their families. (4) Children should be made aware of Al-

Anon and Alateen programs if they are dealing with an alcoholic parent. They should be encouraged to go to these meetings. (5) Girls should be made especially aware of the dangers of speed or CMA as a weight-loss drug. (6) These young adults should be encouraged to reject any powdered substance. (7) As we will see in later chapters, there must be a coordinated effort to address the sources of mental distress and anxiety in the gay and bisexual community for any prevention methods to take hold. (8) The gay community needs to do a better job to get funding for activities for men in their early twenties who see bars and clubs as the only organizing principle of gay life. That is where the CMA starts. (9) The mental health of the gay community and the way in which the gay community takes care of itself must change. The way in which combat veterans create programs for others of their kind who suffer from PTSD should be a model for potential programs in the gay community. We must not underestimate the difficulty that the individual gay adult and the gay community has when it comes to discrimination, anxiety, stigmatization, harassment, HIV fatigue, and legitimate symptoms of PTSD. (We will discuss this in later chapters).

DEATH STUDY: WHAT CAN WE LEARN? AS NIGHT FOLLOWS DAY, CMA BRINGS HIV

1. The dead gay men began using alcohol and drugs sooner at 12–13 years of age. They also began to use CMA by 20 or so. Those most at risk will begin showing drug-taking behavior by 11–13 years of age. Drug education should start in junior high. Discussion of mental disorders also should begin with this group.
2. Their average age when they first used CMA was about 23. They had barely finished high school when they were using hard-core drugs. They were probably in blue-collar jobs or in illegal activity, that is, prostitution, drug dealing, or petty theft. Recall that almost half of them had felony convictions. Programs should work closely with the court system to create awareness of the dangers of CMA and also when it comes to forming better responses to treatment programs for CMA. In the larger gay population, Latino and African American men between the ages of 23–26 (fresh college grads of those right out of graduate school) are most at risk for trying CMA for the first time.
3. The use of heavier drugs such as Ecstasy (X), ketamine (K), GHB (G), heroin, and benzodiazepines by the dead men was coincident with the initiation of CMA. In other words, few if any of them reported abusing X, G, or K before they started using CMA. This is too consistent to be

an accident. CMA is the gateway drug into a combination of other dangerous drugs. The legal and social crackdown must focus on CMA over the other drugs.

4. Infection with HIV occurred shortly after they began using CMA. There was little if any HIV infection before the use of CMA. There should be no doubt that CMA is a gateway drug to HIV, hepatitis, unemployment, and many other life-altering negative consequences.
5. Begin education and law enforcement efforts with regard to CMA among average gay men (and bisexuals) in their early teens through schools. This will go far in reducing both the spread of HIV as well as more dangerous drugs such as GHB, heroin, and ketamine.
6. Developing drug prevention programs that focus on reducing abuse of GHB, ketamine, Ecstasy, or Xanax makes little sense without talking about CMA.
7. Since CMA seems to be an organizing principle in the gay party scene, communicate a strong harm reduction message to discourage CMA use, even if youth wish to experiment with less dangerous drugs such as alcohol, Ecstasy, or cocaine.
8. Join forces with gay or "mixed" clubs to become a part of the solution by allowing advertising to show the dangers of CMA. This advertising should be via posters in bathroom and entrances, bus stops, and after-hour clubs. Ads on bar napkins can be used.
9. It seems that the most vulnerable time for gay men for both CMA and HIV is about 24–27 years of age. Communities should think about programs aimed at this slice of the demographic. This younger element of urban cities does not get enough attention since the focus is on the elderly, the already sick, or those already in rehab. Prevention programs need to target the average 25 year old gay man. (We will see later how this can be done.)
10. It is increasingly accepted that people trying to quit CMA should seriously consider attending three months of rehab to gain several tools for recovery. These include skills learned through cognitive behavioral therapy (CBT), trauma therapy, writing out time lines, group and individual therapy, and Twelve Step work. Well known experts in this field such as Dr. Steve Shoptaw at UCLA now believe that a minimum stay of three months in a facility is not just ideal but required. This is especially true of men who slam CMA, as this is a far deeper level of addiction than snorting or smoking. The outcomes from outpatient programs or Twelve Step programs without any long term initial in-patient facility are very poor, indeed. It is about time we stop skirting around this issue and face the facts. My own anecdotal experience with CMA users suggests that recovery rates without long-term care are less than 5 percent. Men in recovery

from slamming crystal meth have a harder time because their euphoric recall is so much more powerful than those who snort or smoke it.

11. The effect of slamming versus snorting is thought to be least 50 times more powerful. In my experience, men who slam and then want to stop need to be in a rehab facility for at least three months. In this regard, Dr. Steve Shoptaw's views make perfect sense. We need to be upfront about men who slam CMA and try to get sober merely through outpatient programs or through Twelve Step meetings have a high rate of failure. There is no use skipping around this reality, since telling them that Twelve Step programs or outpatient programs are enough only adds to frustration when these attempts are often met with failure. Far more structured treatment is needed to distance a gay man from the powerful urges driven by euphoric recall. A complete break from his former life is needed—social, relationships, physical, cell phone numbers. Everything!

NOTES

1. This was an unpublished study which was part of a large-scale drug treatment program led by Dr. Steve Shoptaw, Ph.D. at UCLA. It was a multi-year treatment for gay and bisexual men to help them to stop CMA abuse. The purpose of this unpublished study was to use public death records from the State of California to discover how and why some of the men died in order to improve treatment programs in the future.

2. T. Kirby and M. Thornber-Dunwell, "High-Risk Drug Practices Tighten Grip on London Gay Scene," *Lancet* 381, no 9861 (January 2013): 101.

3. R. C. Berg and M. W. Ross, "The Second Closet: A Qualitative Study of HIV Stigma Among Seropositive Gay Men in a Southern U.S. City," *International Journal of Sexual Health,* online publication date October 18, 2013.

4. T. J. Starks, H. J. Rendina, A. S. Breslow, J. T. Parson, and S. A. Golub, "The Psychological Cost of Anticipating HIV Stigma for HIV-Negative Gay and Bisexual Men," *AIDS and Behavior* 17, no. 8 (2013): 2732–41; online publication date October 1, 2013.

5. R. L. Findling, B. L. Gracious, N. K. McNamara, E. A. Youngstrom, C. A. Demeter, L. A. Branicky, and J. R. Calabrese, "Rapid, Continuous Cycling and Psychiatric Co-Morbidity in Pediatric Bipolar I Disorder," *Bipolar Disorders* 3, no. 4 (August 2014): 202–10.

6. For this study, that 8 percent of the gay men had bipolar disorder reinforces the unpleasant but highly relevant issue of elevated instances of disorders among gay men. The introduction of this book explained why such disorders are so common among this population. In fact, many people refer to the disease of alcoholism as a *dis*-ease caused by the alcoholic who "hates being in their own skin."

7. Kay Redfield Jamison, "To Know Suicide," *New York Times*, August 20, 2014.

8. M. P. Marshal, Mark S. Friedman, Ron Stall, K. M. King, J. Miles, M. A. Gold, O. G. Bukstein, and J. Q. Morse, "Sexual Orientation and Adolescent Substance Use: A Meta-Analysis and Methodological Review," *Addiction* 103, no. 4 (2008): 546–56.

9. Kay Redfield Jamison, "To Know Suicide," NY Times, August 20, 2014

10. T. Kirby, Michelle Thornber-Dunwell, High-Risk Drug Practices Tighten Grip on London Gay Scene, *Lancet* 381, no. 9861 (January 2013): 101–102.

11. This was taken from discussions with Dr. Steve Shoptaw. While the numbers are somewhat shocking, they should come as no surprise given the cascading effects that drugs like GHB, CMA, and ecstasy gay men have during sex. This combination of drug-taking creates an environment where most studies now conclude that there is a very high chance of men having unsafe sex and thus proliferating HIV transmission.

Chapter Three

The "Down Low"

Bisexual Man and His Haunted Life

Males do not represent two discrete populations, heterosexual and homosexual. The world is not to be divided into sheep and goats. The human mind invents categories and tries to force facts into separate pigeon-holes. The living world is a continuum. . . . The sooner we learn this concerning human sexual behavior the sooner we shall reach a sounder understanding of the realities of sex.

—Kinsey, Pomeroy, and Martin,
Sexual Behavior in the Human Male, 1948

THE DIVIDED AND ALIENATED BISEXUAL MAN

There is probably no more conflicted a person that the bisexual man. We live in a culture where the ultimate stereotype is the dominant alpha male. He is the conqueror, the ruler, the one to be feared. So many of our male cultural icons are masculine, rugged, and "quick on the draw" and they get the beautiful woman in the end. They don't get the woman *and* the man in the end. The list of bisexual icons in literature, Hollywood, or myth is not a long one. To many heterosexual men, being a bisexual is a kind of betrayal of those masculine values of the straight man.

The bisexual man is like the double agent. He risks being exposed by both sides. The gay male lover feels jilted when he finds out the bisexual man has a women or a wife. He wonders why the man does not have the courage to 'come out' as fully gay. The gay man has made profound sacrifices by taking a stand and publicly declaring his homosexuality. He asks why the bisexual man can't have the same level of honesty and take a stand as well. The male lover feels like a sucker for falling for a guy who can't make up his mind.

And the wife or girlfriend feels betrayed and demands retribution when she finds out that the man has had sexual intercourse with another man. She is ashamed and may feel like a fool for not seeing it all along. And she may often blame herself and ask, "Was it me who turned him gay?" She will often see no way to salvage the relationship and may want a quick end to it.

In the world of gay and bisexual addiction, there is an added or heightened sense of skewed perception. The internal word of so many gay and bisexual men is now or was in the past a world of legitimate threats of expulsion from the group, bullying, physical violence, or incarceration. All gay and bisexual men have access to Internet sites such as CNN.com. The front page of this site in 2014 had a story of two men in Iran who were hanged in public—and their hangings were there for millions to see—for being gay.

Does this leave a depressing chill down the spine of a gay man in a free city such as London, San Francisco, or New York? Of course it does. It most definitely leaves a mark even though these men do not live in Tehran or the twelve other countries which execute men for being gay. And they certainly are aware of the almost eighty countries globally where it is a serious crime to be gay. So many gay men I know have to consider anti-homosexual laws when considering vacations to exotic locations. And this is 2014.

In her fascinating book "A Trip to Echo Springs," Olivia Laing traces the lives of famous authors who were alcoholic. She notes that four of the six American winners of the Nobel Prize for Literature were alcoholic. Two were gay and one was bisexual. In her analysis of the talented writer John Cheever—who was bisexual and did eventually get sober in AA toward the end of his life—she described how the dark secret of his bisexuality created profound anxiety for Cheever:

"Cheever lived in the painful knowledge that his erotic desires included men, that these desires were antagonistic and even fatal to the social security he also craved and that as such 'every comely man, every bank clerk and delivery boy was aimed at my life like a loaded pistol.'"

Is it any wonder that in his early twenties, he had experienced self-disgust and sometimes raised the possibility of suicide. Laing adds, "Who wouldn't drink in a situation like that, to ease the pressure of maintaining such intricately folded double lives?[1] Indeed, Cheever's own wife said later in life that she knew he was bisexual, she never mentioned it and also said that John Cheever was "terrified of it himself" (p. 48).

Laing notes that two of the most famous plays of twentieth century America were "A Streetcar Named Desire" and "Cat on a Hot Tim Roof." Both were made into movies that are in the anthology of American cinema. Interestingly, both touch on bisexuality. Blanche Dubois' husband Allen Grey was bisexual and he committed suicide after she caught him in bed with another man. Brick's character (played perfectly by Paul Newman) was considered to be bisexual, though he inferred that his friendship with Skipper (who committed suicide for obscure reasons) was a pure and clean friendship and not "dirty."

It was Brick the alcoholic who was the inspiration for the book's title, for the liquor cabinet was called Echo Spring. And Brick would take "little short trips" to Echo Spring to silence the voices and to obliterate troubled thoughts. The tension in the play is all about the consequences to himself and his marriage to Maggie (played by Elizabeth Taylor) *if* Brick did, indeed, have a sexual affair with Skipper. We do not really know why Skipper commits suicide, but the implication is that he could not live with himself because of his love for Brick. We will never know.

This literary diversion is important because Laing has picked up and examined an often skipped over element to the alcoholism of so many men. This arises from a sense of conflicted sexuality.

Such is the plight of the bisexual man. He is a man who is drained by a life of duplicity and betrayal. He is disliked by the straight man and is seen as betraying the straight male community. He is seen as a liar and a cheat by the woman he loves who wants retribution after she discovers he is sleeping with men. And he is seen as weak and indecisive by a gay man for not having the courage to "come out" of the closet as any 'self-respecting' gay man should. Is it any wonder why recent data shows that bisexual men have rates of addiction which are higher than gay men?

For this is a man whose identity is twice removed. He adheres to the masculine rules of society and has all the heterosexual traits required of the "straight society." But there is a part of himself that enjoys and takes pleasure in loving a man as well. He cannot declare his love for the man because he is attached to a woman and he lives in mortal fear of being discovered by the wife or the girlfriend. So, his encounters with men are often in dark and undesirable places which reinforce his sense of the illicit nature of his desires. It is a downward spiral of shame.

This double life causes confusion, alienation and anxiety. People drink alcohol or take drugs in order to change the way they feel about circumstances they find unacceptable. A bisexual man has a lifestyle fraught with danger, anxiety, and the risk of rejection or expulsion by both the man and the woman. He is a man in a tangle and is often uptight, angry, or checked out. In my years of working with men in recovery, I am convinced there are an inordinately high number of bisexual men who find that alcohol and drugs help to quell the voices and the internal conflict described above. In addition, the men who use drugs such as CMA find themselves often in sexual activity with men. A source of deep shame for some of these men is having sex with other men in a "pay for play" scenario in order to fund their drug-taking behaviors. A sizable group of men in recovery need to be able to talk about this bisexual activity in a safe environment in order to deepen and maintain their sobriety.

BISEXUALITY IN HISTORY: EVERY MAJOR CIVILIZATION CELEBRATED IT. OURS SHOULD TOO

Bisexuality is not some shameful handicap that should be shoved under the carpet. It has been celebrated as a central archetype in the culture and mythology of civilizations for thousands of years. We see it in Babylonian kings, Egyptian gods, Greek warriors, English royalty, Italian artists, and Macedonian rulers. Here are just a few examples which have been handed down for centuries.

Gilgamesh and Enkidu. Erotic and platonic love is a central theme in Gilgamesh, one of the most famous books of ancient times and a predecessor to the Bible. Enkidu is Gilgamesh's lover and is transformed from a wild man into a noble one because of his love for Gilgamesh. Their friendship transforms Gilgamesh from a tyrant into a great king and hero. Enkidu helps Gilgamesh with his restless energy. Gilgamesh helps to extract Enkidu from his selfishness. Gilgamesh's connection to Enkidu makes it possible for Gilgamesh to identify with his people. Their love for each other makes Gilgamesh a better man. When Enkidu dies, Gilgamesh's grief causes him to embark on a futile quest for immortality. After the death of Enkidu, Gilgamesh returns to Uruk on the throne next to his wife Ishtar. He is crushed by the death of his beloved Enkidu, but life goes on.

David and Jonathan. After David kills Goliath in the Valley of Elah and routs the Philistine army, he is brought to King Saul where he meets Saul's son Jonathan. The two form a deep friendship. Jonathan loved David as he loved himself. Jonathan and David cared deeply about each other in a way that was arguably more tender and intimate than a platonic friendship. Jonathan's 'love' for David was chosen over the 'love' of women and is considered evidence for same-sex attraction. The "choosing" (bahar) may indicate a permanent choice and firm relationship. Throughout the Book of Samuel, David and Jonathan consistently reaffirm their love for one another, and Jonathan is willing to turn his back on his father, family, wealth, and traditions for David. Both of them have numerous romantic female interests as well. In a later battle, Jonathan is killed in battle and David laments that Jonathan's love 'was more wonderful than the love of women.'

Horus and Seth. This rivalry between the Egyptian Gods Horus and Seth is about Seth attempting to seduce his rival Horus. Seth displays bisexual characteristics in other fragmentary texts as well, commenting "how lovely your backside is!" to his rival Horus. Seth invites Horus to a feast at his home, and when evening arrives, both of them make a bed and lay down together. That night, they engage in sex. It is important to remember that these two figures are wrapped up in the central families of Egyptian mythology. After all, the mother of Horus is Isis, the main goddess of love and marriage. It is another of many stories in which the historical narrative of the day goes out of its way to discuss bisexuality.

Achilles and Patroclus. Achilles is seen as one of the greatest warriors in all of history. The relationship between Achilles and Patroclus is presented as loving and sexual. They had a devout union 'between the thighs.' Also, both sleep with women. Achilles even gave Patroclus a slave girl as his own in one of his conquests. Plato describes their love for each other as divinely approved. When Patroclus is killed in battle, Achilles is inconsolable and vows revenge on Troy for the death of Patroclus. He is warned that his quest for revenge will cost him his life, but he does not care. The death of his lover Patroclus must be avenged. Achilles is killed by Paris. It is interesting that a story as ubiquitous as the myth of Troy and the Trojan Horse has as its central character someone who is bisexual. Had Patroclus not been killed, we may have never heard of Troy. In fact, the cover of this book is a tribute to Achilles and Patroclus!

The bisexual man seeks authenticity from both men and women but seemingly can't find it because neither should find out. He cannot be his real self. He cannot be authentic. He is a divided self and has a confused identity. This confusion and anxiety often makes it easier for him to pose as a caricature of himself—macho, assured, together. Inside, however, he is a divided self and feels he has a mistaken identity, since what others think of him (both men and women) is fiction. He is neither straight nor gay. He wants to communicate something real and authentic but knows deep down that this is impossible. No wonder drugs and alcohol seem like a viable alternative for him.

We can better understand the need and desire for bisexual men to gravitate toward drugs and alcohol if we look at their private lives and private thoughts. In the following section, we will go into the dark alleys and seedy bars in order to see the darkness in their lives. We will see how their secretive lives and shameful self-image translates into self-destructive activity and how this activity has profound consequences for the other people in their lives.

We will also see how their rejection from community and church causes them to play out their low self-image and low self-esteem as they are told that their bisexuality is evil, immoral, or plain wrong. They sublimate their sexuality and end up in situations which are unhealthy for everyone. We will see that when society condemns what they consider a natural part of themselves, they go down a dark path of sexual activity which is risky and degrading for them and others.

THE BISEXUAL "DOWN LOW" MAN AND HIV TRANSMISSION

A few female doctors with whom I worked during my internship at UCLA sought to find out what makes these bisexual men tick. They wanted to know their attitudes toward HIV and sexual patterns with transvestites and transsexuals. They wanted to know, in particular, what was behind the spread of HIV in the heterosexual community. The study focused on a group of people most at risk for HIV infection and who can also spread HIV into the heterosexual population—namely, "down low" (DL) bisexual men.[2] These are men who have female wives, partners, or casual sexual acquaintances but who also have sex with men at least one time every three months. This group is predominantly African American and Latino but also included white males.

The study began by interviewing social workers who work with straight men and women to get a sense of the typical heterosexual patterns of sexual activity. Then the researchers turned their attention to understanding the patterns and types of sexual behavior common among cross-dressers and male-to-female (MTF) transgender people by interviewing leaders of these small communities. Lastly, the researchers surveyed men who identify as heterosexual but occasionally have sex with gay men, cross-dressers, or transgender people.

In total, more than thirty heterosexual men who reported having occasional sex with men or MTF transgender people were interviewed. Half of these men reported that they were heterosexual but infrequently had sex with gay men; 30 percent reported that they had sex with transgender people; and 20 percent reported having sex with both men and transgender people (male-to-female). Many of these men were HIV positive. They reported that they were "often" unsafe with their gay or transgender partner. They also reported that they were "generally" safe with their female partners. In addition, they reported their HIV status to their female partners but "often" did not disclose their status to the gay or transgender partner.[3]

The findings of this study open up a can of worms for many of the subgroups that were being examined. For example: (1) Who are the female partners who remain with these men when the male partner discloses various details of sexual activity that would put the female at risk for sexually transmitted diseases or HIV? (2) Why would gay or transgender men put themselves at risk for contracting HIV by having unprotected sex with DL partners when they would undoubtedly heard in the community that they may have HIV? (3) How much of this activity is "pay for play?" And, (4) What is the fascination with transgender people by DL heterosexuals, considering half of this admittedly small sample had a preference for transgender people?[4]

The men in this study are predominantly ethnic minorities, including Latino and African American men, who had received a high school education. Most were in their thirties, were unmarried, and were living either alone or with a roommate. About 40 percent of these men had themselves engaged in prostitution. One-third had been sexually abused when they were younger. More than half were currently abusing drugs. These men were mostly "tops" although some were "bottoms." And they engaged in oral sex as well.

Regarding sexual partners, most of the men preferred MTF transgender people with their penis still attached. Much of this activity was "pay for play"; that is, prostitution. The men met their sexual partners in three ways: on the street, "online" through dating sites that catered to their particular predilection, or in gay bathhouses. The type of sex they often preferred was described as "dark, kinky, or rough" and was often accompanied by drug use. The sex was often a quick "pickup" and anonymous. These men engaged in this behavior about once a month or slightly less.[5]

As we begin to piece together this puzzle, a few questions arise. What do men or transgender people with their penises attached offer that a women cannot? The answer here is simple. The men who were interviewed said that men are "horn dogs" and are "ready" for sex more frequently than women. They found that, by and large, other men found casual and anonymous sex more acceptable than women did. They also reported that men were "better" at oral sex than women. In short, they reported that men and transgender people are "easier," better at oral sex, and more open to anonymous sex. In addition, male partners would agree to anal sex, which they found more stimulating than vaginal sex. Later in this chapter, we will see that there is more to this story, but in general the heterosexual DL male prefers to have sex with gay or transgender men primarily for "convenience"—quick, anonymous, and easy sex. According to these study participants, women simply do not accommodate men with "easy and quick" sex as readily as gay or transgender men do.

Now that we have more information, we can circle back and answer a few of the earlier questions:

Why do women tolerate male partners who put them at risk by engaging in "pay for play" sex with gay or transgender men from a high-risk group (sex workers or people who have sex in bathhouses or alleys)? The answer is simple. These men were not fully honest with their female partners. They would often describe their activity with men as "a phase" or something that was "in the past" and which they were no longer doing. Nonetheless, these men often reported that they would use condoms with their female partners and the women would obviously accept these conditions. Conversely, they would not reveal their HIV status with their male sexual partners. They preferred to "top" without using a condom.

Why do gay men and transgender people allow these DL heterosexual men to be the insertive top? Down low men typically think there is not a problem being a top without a condom because they assume their gay and transgender partners are already HIV positive, so why bother wearing a condom? They may be aware of their HIV status or do not bother to check. The gay and transgender men, on the other hand, assume "straight" men are HIV negative, so why bother wearing a condom? Hence, a ticking time bomb with both groups. They are both making fatally flawed assumptions of the other group based on ignorant stereotypes.

What meaning do they derive from these encounters? This also covers question 4 above about the fascination with transgender people.

Money. Several of these DL bisexual men were from a lower income group and would sometimes sell their bodies to other men for oral and anal sex to make money. Often, they said they would allow a gay man to perform oral sex on them and that they would be the "top." In their mind, the "pay for play" also excuses the behavior because they are doing it for money rather than pleasure.

Undesirable to women. Some of the men commented that they see themselves as "undesirable" to women because of their bisexuality. They believe that their bisexuality makes them less than a real man, and so they seek out cross-dressers or transgender people (with penis attached) rather than women to alleviate the shame of being attracted to men.

Desire for the unnatural. Some of the other men reported seeing sex with a cross-dresser or transgender person as an exotic thrill, a "high like parachuting." They comment on the excitement of having sex with a person who "screams like a woman but cums like a man." Others said it was a turn-on simply because it is "unnatural or wrong." So, there is a dark element to the sex—its "forbidden" nature makes it all the more enticing to some. Perhaps the men feel they are "wrong" so the sex must be viewed as wrong in order to produce an "added high." Furthermore, these DL men reported that cross-dressers or transgender men are more open to "kinky sex." It is a chance to be dirty ("water sports"), rough ("S&M"), kinky ("sex toys")—fantasies that would not be tolerated at home. These down low men report that "men are more sexually open than woman!"[6]

These bisexual men who have sex with women report that gay and transgender men "know how to give pleasure to other males." They report that receiving oral sex from a male and being a top with a male feels better than being with a woman. The cross-dressers and transgender men are more eager to please. Furthermore, these sexual acts are fairly immediate and do not involve the extended negotiations they report having with a female partner, experiences described as "labor-intensive, expensive, politically complicated" and the female partners described as "nags" or who "play hard to get."[7]

Fidelity maintained. Other men said they had sex with cross-dressers or transgender men because they were not "real" women and thus their sexual liaisons could not be considered infidelity. According to this viewpoint, these sexual partners who are not really women are "disposable," allowing the man to return to his female partner with a clean conscience. In this way, "fidelity" is maintained. Although this appears to be a game of semantics, we will see that words really do matter and that these men can use words to create all kinds of illusions about their masculinity.

We have to ask, Is this about semantics or are there genuinely different cultural norms for how men in different countries look at sex? One study made a prescient point that in Mexico, for instance, a male's masculine gender identity is not threatened by homosexual acts as long as he plays the inserter sex role; only the male insertee, playing a female sex role, is considered homosexual. An analysis of the Mexican data suggested that bisexual behavior is more easily accepted in Mexico. This study put the level of bisexuality in Mexico at about 30 percent.[8]

The bottom line is this: These men are horny! They want it now; they want it rough; and they want it kinky if that can be arranged. Drugs and alcohol reduce their inhibitions and increase their horniness. To preserve the illusion of fidelity, they hook up with gay and transgender men—sexual partners who are more accessible, "cheap and easy," and free of intimacy, attachment, and obligation. Their sexual encounters are quick, anonymous, and "feel good for five minutes." There is no connection, emotion, or intimacy involved, and they have no respect for their sexual partner.

This leads to a thorny issue. Several of the reasons these men give to explain why they have sex with a gay man, cross-dresser, or transgender person revolve around convenience, ease of meeting, and immediate satisfaction. However, these criteria could also be satisfied by visiting a female prostitute, women who are convenient, easy to meet, and provide immediate gratification. In this light, these criteria should be considered secondary to the primary consideration that the men receive a certain "high" from having sex with a man, a man dressed like a women, or, to use the defamatory term many of these men used, "she-males." Indeed, in my work counseling gay men in treatment from the upper echelons of society, I have heard many say that sex with a transgender person is the "ultimate freaky high." They report that it is the height of strangeness and, many have said, the ultimate high when combined with drugs, usually cocaine and CMA. Furthermore, a study in India that interviewed men who have sex with men in four south Indian states found that almost half of the men who had sex with other men and transgender people were married to women. Many of these same men also reported visiting female prostitutes.[9] If this is not a vindication of the Kinsey study, nothing is.

Discussions with transgender people in recovery help us understand how this dynamic gets started. For example, one of the leaders of the transgender community in a large metropolitan city pointed out that because transgender people have little acceptance in society, they often are forced to work as prostitutes—they simply can't find jobs because of their physical appearance. The men who gravitate to MTF transgender people receive sexual gratification and heightened stimulation not available from a female sex partner. Their sexual liaisons may also include meeting both passive gay men and cross-dressers. All such activity often includes the use drugs and/or alcohol. This dynamic may satisfy both the financial needs of transgender people, who find it difficult to obtain regular work, and the needs of bisexual men who may be carrying around a shameful secret.

When asked how they felt after these encounters, the men in the study said they felt "dirty" or "ashamed." They reported wanting to "slow down" or "stop" their behavior altogether. It was something they felt was unacceptable or that they would be ostracized for if they were caught. The word "sinful" came up frequently. They reported that these feelings of bisexuality caused "guilt, remorse" and that these encounters made them feel depressed.

Strong religious beliefs (often these are childhood beliefs of a punishing God that are carried into adulthood) may create a conflicted self. These bisexual men have desires to engage in sexual activity with men who have a penis (cross-dressers or transgender men) but believe this sexual activity is wrong. Many seek forgiveness through prayer after they have entered the "dark side" or have "fallen from heaven." They often refer to themselves as "fallen angels." There is a powerful religious component in their shame; several of them said they often pray not to repeat the behavior.[10]

Religious mores of the community that condemn homosexuality—combined with the social mores of a heterosexual-dominated society—seemed to be a double weight around their necks. This behavior was "unmanly" and "sinful." According to this view, to be gay is one thing but to be straight (more or less) and then to have sex with cross-dressers or transgender people is a violation of both religious mores (which condemn homosexuality) and social mores. We can see now why one word arose so frequently in conversations with these men: they felt "tortured." Further, they reported feeling haunted by a "dark or evil" side and feeling "angry or filthy" because of their desires for men "in various forms."

So, what they consider to be natural feelings and compulsions for these types of sexual encounters are considered both "unmanly" and sinful by society. If they were found out, this would be a source of shame perhaps more disturbing than if a closeted gay person was found out. With the case of a bisexual man being discovered with a cross-dresser or transgender man, the heterosexual response may essentially be "Hey, we thought you were one of us." Yet the typical heterosexual response to a gay man being discovered with another man is essentially "To each his own!" or even "It figures. We thought so!"

This is not just an Anglo-Saxon phenomenon. A study in India of four states with high rates of HIV showed a significant bisexual cross-section. Almost half of the men surveyed had female partners. Many of them had sex with transgender and gay men (paid and unpaid) and then had sex with women (paid and unpaid). The Hindi word for transgender is *Hijira*. The Hindi word for bottom is *Kothi,* and a sexually versatile man is referred to as a "double-decker." India is currently debating a law that makes homosexual activity illegal.[11] Yet, interestingly, in mid-2014 the government of India officially recognized transgender people's right to claim legal identity on government identification as a third gender. This occurred at a time when the Indian high court was trying to strike down laws offering equal treatment to gays. All too often, the movement to offer dignity to gays and lesbians is a "two steps forward, one step back" process.

GAY AND BISEXUAL BEHAVIORS AROUND THE WORLD: THE GLOBAL STATISTICS

One of the largest meta-studies on bisexuality in the emerging world was by prevalence of bisexuality among men who were polled in a meta-study done which combined 561 studies. Suffice it to say that this is one of the most detailed studies on global bisexuality ever conducted.[1] It is interesting to note that the highest prevalence of bisexuality is in Latin America while the lowest is in East Asia. The upper range of Latino men who reported having bisexual experiences was about 20 percent. Eastern Europe also reported that they had fairly high levels of bisexuality with the numbers reaching an upper range of 15 percent. SE Asia also had high levels of bisexuality where the range of those reporting bisexual experiences reached 12 percent. Northeast Asia had the lowest self-reported levels of bisexuality in the emerging world with the range no higher than 5 percent.

Note

1. C. Cáceres, K. Konda, M. Pecheny, A. Chatterjee, and R. Lyerla. "Estimating the Number of Men Who Have Sex with Men in Low and Middle Income Countries," *Sexually Transmitted Infections,* March 2006; (a metastudy of 561 studies). (Prevalence of high-risk sex among MSM in South Asia was 70–90 percent and 40–60 percent for the rest.)

THE PLIGHT OF THE BISEXUAL MAN

The reflections and comments from this group of bisexual men have some important implications. It is just as important to recognize and encourage those who are bisexual to reconcile themselves with their feelings and actions as it is for gay men and lesbians to reconcile themselves to their feelings and actions. In some ways, the plight of a bisexual man is more problematic because he has an added layer of guilt. One layer is that he feels evil because he prefers to have sex with other men over women, and the other is that he is "unmanly" because he is not 100 percent heterosexual. This is particularly true in the Latino culture, which has both a strong tradition of "macho" masculinity as well as deep sense of Catholic religiosity. Disconnecting feelings of "being evil" and "feeling guilty" from natural feelings of bisexuality is one important goal of drug-taking behavior, since drugs are often used to drown out feelings of shame, guilt, self-loathing, and remorse. It is a vicious cycle where drugs (and drug-fueled promiscuity) cause self-loathing and the remedy for that self-loathing is more drugs.

In this mysterious mix of sexual activity, drugs and alcohol cause, as it is known in the scientific community, a "deviation in regular sex protocol." That is, drugs may make people desire "freaky sex"—the freakier the better. Drugs increase sex drive and reduce inhibitions. This is most true with cocaine and crystal meth. Almost 80 percent of the men in this study were drug takers who were using some combination of alcohol, cocaine, and CMA. So, many of these man who identify as heterosexuals and who are regularly tops often become bottoms while on these drugs. They then blame the drug for their behavior, claiming, "The meth made me do it!" (A vast amount of literature does support the theory that CMA causes them to become a bottom.) Not surprisingly, however, they then question their masculinity, since what kind of heterosexual man would agree to be a bottom?

Furthermore, these men admit they would visit bathhouses while using drugs like cocaine and CMA and engage in sexual activity with several partners. They often prefer to visit a bathhouse or sauna because they do not like gay bars, arguing that "gay bars are for 'faggots'—not me." They would also seek out transgender sex and, no matter their male partner, skip condom use. That seems to explain how these men contracted HIV in the first place. High on CMA, these men engaged in anal-receptive sex without any protection. Some of them said they contracted HIV from oral sex, although the chances of this are quite low and the reasoning dubious.[12]

Again, whether it is meeting in a bar, in a sauna, or through the Internet, the encounter is depersonalized and the person is objectified. It is a matter of "shut up and f*ck." The sex is immediate and finished quickly. The person then leaves. There is a sense that the encounter can be denied due to its speed. A few of the men in the study even said that other "men who have sex with men are bisexual. I am not." They see the anus of the transgender person as a "female sex object," and so consider this sex to be heterosexual in nature. Gay people often view such denial as a sign that the bisexual man is actually a closet gay person. This is a cause of much rancor in bisexual literature.

Yet, there is something genuinely bisexual going on when a man has sex with a transgender person. These men seem to be attracted to the feminine qualities and to embrace the female identity of the transgender person. Some of them commented that they liked being with someone who was "pretty and smelled nice, someone who was feminine." This seems to ease their sense of conflict.

These men may feel conflicted or even tortured because, while they generally prefer sex with a woman, a part of them truly desires sex with a man. This may cause them to use the word "sissy" to describe a gay person. They feel forced by society to compartmentalize the part of themselves that desires men. This part is turned into a painful secret that has no outlet except through clandestine encounters, which are quick, depersonalized, raunchy, and can lead to the kind of self-loathing that breeds alcohol dependence.

The distorted identity of the bisexual man described above is often referred to as bi-phobia. Further, some believe that bisexuality is not real. That is referred to as bi-erasure—the minimization and dismissal of bisexuality as a real phenomenon. The *New York Times* reviewed eleven surveys and found that "among adults who identify as L.G.B., bisexuals comprise a slight majority." In one of the larger surveys, 3.1 percent of American adults identified as bisexual, while 2.5 percent identified as gay or lesbian. We will see later that the incidence of alcohol and drug dependence for bisexual men is at least as high as that of gay men.

Unlike gay men, bisexual men are seen as an invisible group and have yet to "come out of the closet." The survey results are all over the place, but only about one in five bisexual men identify explicitly as bisexual. And some surveys among high school students show that young adults are willing to identify as something other than heterosexual or gay. In one survey, 13 percent of non-heterosexual young adults were willing to identify as something other

MARK'S STORY: DO HETEROSEXUAL MEN 'BECOME' BISEXUAL WHEN THEY USE CMA?

Here is a story of how Twelve Step programs for crystal meth and sex allowed one man to come back from the brink. Mark is a forty-eight-year-old gay British man who first started snorting crystal meth at the age of nineteen in order to work longer shifts at a grocery store. He came out as gay at about the same time but had sex with both straight and gay men while on crystal meth. It is important to remember that Mark is not really a drinker and never was, though his parents are both alcoholics. He was primarily a crystal meth user. He stopped for a while and finished university only to pick up meth again in the mid-1990s while working in New York City. By 1998, meth began to get the better of him and he would go on two- to three-day binges and have sex with as many as six or seven partners during one binge. He was continually missing work and finally was offered a severance package.

Mark spent many years on meth and, when high, was sexual with many different people in various circumstances. He commented, "There is no sexual identity when someone is on meth." As Mark described it, straight men who would never kiss another man will become bottoms and perform oral sex on another man when on meth, and straight women will participate in lesbian sex. Sexual activity becomes twisted, with examples ranging from S&M to simulated crucifixion to incest fantasies and gang-banging. Users report that when one is on meth, twelve hours seems like a minute. Meth is a pure fantasy drug that allows the user to release all guilt and inhibition. Crystal meth was definitely a sex drug for Mark and it allowed him to explore a range of fantasies with dozens of partners.

The problem with meth, he said, was that in the latter stages of abusing the drug, "2 percent of the sex was amazing and 98 percent was a ridiculous effort in chasing a pipe and endless masturbation." He said he could "masturbate until he was dehydrated." When he came down from the high, he felt "disgusted and full of guilt and remorse." He only ever smoked meth and never slammed (used intravenously). As with many CMA users, though, he started using other drugs like GHB, cocaine, ketamine, and ecstasy after he began using meth. By the time he was ready to get help in 1999, there was, he said, only one way to describe his condition: "total despair."

Mark was one of the early pioneers of CMA (Crystal Meth Anonymous) in New York City. When he got sober in 1999, there were only two meetings of CMA in New York. One meeting had only a few members and the most "experienced" had only six months of continuous sobriety. Mark jumped into the CMA program without going to a rehab. He was very active and by the end of his first year, he was sponsoring several guys.

Mark thinks that about 15 percent of the people in CMA meetings in 2000 were slamming. Today, he believes that about 50 percent who enter CMA meetings are slamming. He thinks this is because there is a sense that slamming is "the in thing" because a surprisingly high proportion of the younger guys are doing it. It has taken on a glamorous quality. Mark knows of several people who have had heart attacks and died from slamming.

Mark's experience is that "of the people who come to CMA and stay actively involved, about 50 percent stay around and gather longer-term sobriety." The problem is that most who enter the CMA programs do not get active in the Twelve Step community.

Mark also went to Sex Addicts Anonymous (SAA) when he was five years clean from meth to help him develop a healthy sex life after so many years of twisted fantasy-filled meth sex. He said this was the hardest part of his recovery, and it took five years for him to separate crystal meth sex fantasies from normal sex with a stable partner. It was a long slog to where he is today but he contends that the work was well worth it. Today, Mark has a great job and a long-term partner from Italy. For him, the combination of CMA and SAA did the trick. CMA support groups are thriving in New York City, where there are fifty meetings per week. Despite a growing crystal meth problem in the gay community, Mark sees a definite reason for hope.

than gay, and 8 percent were questioning. Perhaps the younger generation is finding more ease with the fluidity of human sexuality, but the current adult population seems ambivalent at best.

In the eyes of many Americans, bisexuality is a taboo concept that generates discomfort and bewilderment. Some gay men even think it is an invention—that a bisexual is merely a man on his way to coming out as gay. It is really the last frontier of what can loosely be referred to as a misunderstood minority group. Indeed, the American Institute of Bisexuality (AIB) reports that some of the worst discrimination toward bisexual men comes from the gay community. There is a sense in the gay community that can be laid out as follows: "I paid a very high price to come out of the closet. You bisexual men want it both ways. You should have the courage to come out." Yet this does not ring true for most bisexuals. They are simply not gay.[13]

We can see that these men are caught in a mental vice between the gay and straight worlds. Disclosing occasional sex with men threatens their heterosexual relationship. Their wife or female partner may call them gay and/or leave them. They automatically assume that their female partners will feel betrayal, disgust, self-blame, and an assortment of other unpleasant emotions. And since a disruption of the relationship would threaten the man's living arrangement and friendship network, he lies to maintain the illusion of fidelity and heterosexuality. But marital discord is still bound to arise because his partner senses that he is keeping a secret. And just how does the husband explain long absences in evenings or sudden unexplained "meetings?" The husband or partner may accuse his female partner of being "pushy" for asking too many questions.

The man compartmentalizes the behavior and creates another world that is kept secret from his spouse. This can lead to another set of problems; namely, what is true and what is false? He sees the side of him who prefers men as a side that is fraught with trouble, including grave consequences if it is disclosed and a mortal threat to his masculine role in society. A lot is hanging on this closed-off fantasy world, which must remain a secret for the sake of his family, his role in the community, and the accepted sense of his masculinity. He lives a lie. He lives in a world of secrets. Secrets and lies are good kindling for alcohol abuse. Furthermore, he may be forced into the tawdry world of male escorts as the only way to satisfy his secret desires. Many surveys indicate that more than half the clientele of male escorts (and in some cases as much as 80 percent) are *not* gay men but men who are married to women.[14] So, the only option for bisexual men who cannot have a candid, honest, and potentially life-giving discussion about his sexuality with his female partner is to turn to unsafe trysts with street hookers or escorts advertised on the Internet. The risks of such encounters include HIV transmission and STDs as well as another common feature in the gay escort industry—drug and alcohol abuse.[15]

In my own experience counseling former male escorts in recovery for drug dependence (mostly CMA), I have noticed a number of issues. First, many of them say that 60 to 80 percent of their clients are married men and that gay men actually are a small portion of their business. One patient told me, "If it were not for married men, the male escort industry would not exist." Second, the greatest success rate in recovery for men who were male escorts occurred in those who got clean and sober and did not return to the escort trade. Most, if not all, of the men who returned to this line of work ended up relapsing. And no wonder—it is a world littered with alcohol and drugs, including CMA, pot, alcohol, ketamine, amyl nitrate (poppers), and GHB.

In conclusion, we think of the gay and lesbian populations as having a significantly higher proportion of alcohol and drug dependence. However, as research differentiates between men who have sex with women (MSW) and men who have sex with men and women (MSM/W), we can see that in high school, university, and adult life, bisexual men have an even higher incidence of drug and alcohol dependence than gay men. One study showed that among a group of low-income African American and Latino men, the men most

THE SANCTITY OF MARRIAGE: ISN'T SANCTITY ANOTHER WORD FOR HONESTY?

A worthwhile topic on this issue of bisexuality revolves around the sanctity of marriage. In the traditional marriage between one man and one woman, if a man finds himself changing and developing bisexual tendencies (or can no longer repress long-held desires for men), the current mentality suggests he has a few choices: (1) exit the marriage in divorce so as not to create great hurt and feelings of betrayal from the wife; (2) pursue anonymous sex with a lover on the side while staying in the marriage in order to maintain responsibilities as the breadwinner and paymaster for the education of the children and the upkeep of the home; or (3) surreptitiously pick up men in gay bars for quick sex or hire male escorts. It seems, however, that we are currently witnessing the beginnings of movement in society that demands another way out. Basically one option is to leave the marriage and the other is to live a shameful and double life of male escorts and shady bars. Is there a third way? We will discuss this below. Marriage needs to have sanctity but sanctity has honesty as its foundation. Bisexuality is a human phenomenon which has been recorded in literature for more than 5,000 years. Ancient cultures even revered it. It is part of the human experience. To have the admission of bisexuality in a marriage as a total non-starter (or for this result in divorce) seems draconian and belies history, reality and human frailty. The discussion needs to go in a healthier direction for options which allow a man or a woman who has discovered he or she is bisexual to remain in a loving and sanctified marriage.

likely to have a high rate of substance abuse (and remarkably a higher rate of homo-negativity than gay men) were bisexual men.[16] Another study showed that bisexual college men (along with gay men) were two times more likely to have abused Ecstasy in the past year compared to heterosexual men.[17] Lastly, when it comes to being a runaway youth, having drug dependence, or trying to commit suicide, bisexual men rank right up there with gay men. Bisexual women, too, are at high risk for drug dependence.[18]

In 2014, gays, lesbians, and bisexual men continue to face institutionalized prejudice, heightened stress, anxiety, family exclusion, anti-gay hatred, internalized shame, drug and alcohol abuse, and high levels of suicide. Bisexual men are increasingly and rightly seen as a different and discrete group from gays and lesbians, who are at least as likely, if not more, to have problems with drug and alcohol abuse, low self-esteem, suicidality, and internalized self-hatred.[19]

THE TRANS-PARENT CEO

The highest paid female in the United States is a woman named Martine Rothblatt. She has been married for thirty-three years and is the CEO of United Therapeutics. She was one of the founders of Sirius Radio. When her daughter, Jenesis, was seven, she developed a rare, often-fatal heart and lung condition. Martine decided to create a company to find a treatment for her daughter and eventually founded United Therapies. United Therapies now has a market capitalization of $5.4 billion and her daughter is now thirty.

The interesting part of Martine is not the money but that she is a male to female transsexual and a pioneer in thinking about sexuality. Her book called *The Apartheid of Sex* says that there are billions of people in the world and each of them has a unique sexual identity. "Genitals are as irrelevant to one's role in society as skin tone." She suggests we think of sexual identity as a spectrum. On one end could be the aggressive nurturing person who does not try to appear sexy. The middle could be a less aggressive person. And the other end could be gentle, nourishing and erotic person.

Her point is that we should open ourselves to sexuality and see that genitalia do not exclusively define us. The body is but a shell, Martine concludes. The mind and the heart are what count. Martine is a "woman who has been married to the same African-American woman for 33 years and dropped everything to help develop a drug for her daughter." So, "she is a transsexual woman married to a woman, which makes her also, sort of, a lesbian." She defines herself ultimately as a free spirit and believes that "we are all happier when we can express whatever happenstance is in our souls." She lives by two principles: Life offers great purpose and love is essential.[1]

Note

1. Taken from "The Trans-Everything CEO," by Lisa Miller. New York. September 8–21, 2014.

RECOMMENDATIONS

Studies around the world demonstrate that bisexuality is a universal phenomenon and should be celebrated. It is least pronounced in East Asia where, ironically, we do not quickly use the word "macho" to describe East Asian men and most pronounced in Latin America, where, also ironically, we do use the word "macho" to describe Latino men. One of the goals of this chapter has been to explicitly and emphatically describe bisexual behaviors that are universal and for which, when clearly stated, should reduce the levels of shame and embarrassment. The reason is simple. When there is a shared experience and when others can lay out their story, the feelings of isolation and shame tend to fall away and healing can begin. There is a sense of "me too." And the feeling of "no one is as dirty or perverted as I am" also falls away. In this way, people can be more candid and forthright about beginning a dialogue in the following way.

Husbands and wives need to talk about the "mystery" of bisexuality. Too many studies are qualitative studies that focus on motivations and behaviors of bisexual men. We need to question why are there so few studies that focus on the perspectives, biases, and preferences of women who have bisexual boyfriends or husbands. Will they really throw their husbands out if they discover that they find men sexually attractive as well as women? Can a dialogue about bisexuality reduce the fear men have about disclosing this behavior? Does disclosure of bisexual orientation mean the end of a marriage? This is a commonly perceived myth. We need to determine whether it is really true. If women (especially women married to Latino men) think that bisexual behavior stops when the marriage begins, then they may be fooling themselves. Recall the study that showed that as many as 40 percent of Latino men engaged in bisexual activity.

If every married man who was discovered to be bisexual faced an immediate divorce, then millions of marriages would be ending. If nothing else, a dialogue about this issue can go a long way toward reducing HIV transmission as well as the shame and self-loathing that drugs and alcohol seek to smother. Husbands who have bisexual tendencies, but who feel they would be ostracized by their wives if they were found out, will continue to push their feelings underground and pursue a secret-filled life of anonymous (and often unsafe) encounters, which are accompanied by drugs and alcohol. If both the husband and wife conclude that the topic is "too hot to handle," "a forbidden topic," or a "religious taboo," then the marriage is likely in trouble anyway.

The old saying "You are only as sick as your secrets" applies to a couple just as much as it applies to an individual. In the end, only good can come from open and honest dialogue. The kindling for the alcoholic bonfire is secrets and shame. Bisexuality is a perfect intersection for both. The dialogue and the ramifications of the dialogue should be celebrated in safe, life-giving, and respectful ways. An article in Salon.com by Mark Cohen, referenced below, gives ample hope that husbands and wives can maintain and even renew a marriage if the husband reveals bisexuality.

One of the shocking conclusions from the literature on the issue of if and how bisexual should men reveal their sexual secrets to a female partner is actually the absence of research on just what female partners think about all this. The studies on this topic are few and far between. Among the more enlightened studies is one from the *Journal of Bisexuality*. It highlights the "importance of the couple's working together to maintain a satisfying post-disclosure marriage. The relationship of the bisexual husbands and heterosexual wives of bisexual men with their respective spouses was marked by a multileveled interaction that included mutual sexual pleasure, as well as cognitive, verbal, behavioral, and emotional engagement. Their joint effort over time enabled them to deconstruct not only traditional concepts of marriage, but also dichotomous views of sexual orientation." A far wider dialogue is needed on this score. And this dialogue needs to be direct, adult, frank, and candid.[20] In one encouraging study, 64 percent of couples who entered couples counseling after a disclosure of bisexuality remained married.[21]

Why do governments think that outlawing homosexuality will somehow "solve the AIDS problem" or will cause all people to enter into monogamous heterosexual marriages? While it's true that unsafe sex with sex workers or casual sex with bisexuals and their partners is one transmission route for HIV into the heterosexual population, putting gay people or "deviants" in jail will neither stop the spread of HIV nor prevent homosexuality. Such tactics actually have a way of backfiring and could result in unintended consequences that are very expensive for countries. First, two-thirds of the men in the down low male study referenced in the beginning of this chapter spent time in prison. In the absence of an available female, many reported that a male or transgender person was a "good second choice." In other words, in an all-male environment, many of these men deepened their tendency to have sex with transgender men, cross-dressers, or other gay men. As some of these men explained, "I used a man as a woman" because there were no *real* women around. (In fact, a few men in the study said their first bisexual experience with a cross-dresser was actually in prison.) These men clearly had a pragmatic approach to the experience of prison. If a female was not available, they would settle for a gay man or a MTF transgender person who offered them the "caress" of a woman. Second, the rates of HIV transmission among prison populations are alarmingly high. So, putting gay people in prison not only reinforces bisexual tendencies but may increase the spread of HIV.

The main audience for the DL bisexual in the American context should be Latino and African American men. They do not wish to be associated with the white gay world. They need to be recognized and treated as a distinct group. As mentioned earlier, there is greater confusion, anxiety, and pressure about bisexuality (and being gay) in this world given the Catholic influence in Latino culture and the Southern Baptist influence in African American culture. The messages about awareness and help with regard to HIV treatment and prevention, as well as drug and alcohol treatment, need to be presented in a way that appreciates the sensitivities of this group. HIV prevention strategies as well as drug and alcohol treatment for bisexual men should be directed at the heterosexual male world where there are stronger family ties. For example, they could be offered in the office of the family doctor, at community fairs, and at screening events for diabetes or high cholesterol. The bisexual community—and the DL community in particular—need to be treated as a distinct minority group with its own needs. Other areas where advertisements for HIV prevention, as well as drug and alcohol treatment, may be appropriate include street fairs, adult bookstores, and Internet sites. Targeting heterosexual bars where there is a weekly "gay night" is another ideal place to highlight the high prevalence of drug and alcohol dependence for bisexual men.

The issue of gay and bisexual relationships is a sticky wicket when it comes to religious organizations. Shame over being bisexual is only reinforced in Catholic Latino and Southern Baptist African American communities. One study of bisexual men in New York found that these men "evoked beliefs in God in coping with adverse life experiences; and some linked faith to family and sexual responsibilities."[22] For many DL bisexual men, organized religion is an important part of their life. Under the new Pope Francis, the Catholic Church appears to be lightening up on the issue of homosexuality. One issue that needs greater discussion is the way in which intolerance of gay or bisexual orientation drives men into secret and unhealthy lives of shame, self-hatred, and, very often, alcoholism. A more tolerant attitude from the hierarchy of both the Catholic and the Southern Baptist churches would help improve the mental health of thousands of gay and bisexual men who are a reflection—not an abomination—of their creator. As it is, the rate of HIV transmission among southern African American males is rising at rates far in excess of those ethnic groups in other parts of the country. Southern men (both white and African American) need churches that accept them and love them—not ones which expel them.

The gay and transgender communities need education about the issue of HIV prevalence among "straight" men. Though they say they are married and, therefore, should be HIV negative as they are presumed to be "devout" husbands, some of these bisexual men could have contracted HIV. Furthermore, there is even some sensitivity about being seen to "impose" a set of rules and mores about controlling HIV. Groups that try to impose a set of do's and don'ts when it comes to sexual activity can often cause rancor and upset. There is a powerful stigma attached to people who have HIV. These people experience anxiety, loneliness, depression, and suicidal ideations. Some people think that it is perfectly acceptable to be quite aggressive in messages aimed at controlling the spread of HIV. But, recommendations to control the spread of HIV with messages which can have overtones of "knock it off with the meth" or "use a condom, for God's sake" can be seen as aggressive and offensive by those with HIV and even by gay or bisexual men who are HIV negative. This merits sensitivity, especially when addressing the transgender community.[23]

Targeting their female partners, as well as gay and transgender partners, with informational and educational materials is also wise. Let's take two extremes. The main purpose of the study previously mentioned was to examine how HIV was moving into the heterosexual community. This is a deadly serious issue because women were unknowingly being infected by men who were not forthcoming about their risky sexual behavior. One qualitative study highlighted this by analyzing the devastation in women's lives when they discover the HIV status of their husbands. The themes and emotions that were highlighted include anger, betrayal, disillusionment, isolation, denial, and self-blame.[24] On the other hand, Salon.com published a feature article about a bisexual man who came out to his wife. Initially, the wife had similar emotions—betrayal, disillusionment, isolation. Subsequently, however, the couple learned to embrace the husband's bisexuality into the marriage in ways that the couple found life-giving and satisfying. Much work is needed to make wives and female partners aware of the risks of contracting HIV from their husbands and partners. In addition, more research needs to be done on how couples can maintain and even enhance a relationship when the male partner's bisexuality is disclosed.

In conclusion, dare I say that the culture may be changing. More people are recognizing that sexuality must be celebrated in all its forms. There is greater acceptance that ever before, even though there is a long way to go. Western history is full of bisexuality in all its forms. These are not just whimsical stories but powerful myths which are at the center of the history of major civilizations. We have David and Jonathan in Jewish culture. There is Gilgamesh and Enkedu in Persian culture. We have the mighty warrior Achilles and Petroclus in Greek culture. We see Horus and Seth in Egyptian culture. And we have Alexander the Great and Hephaestion in Macedonian culture. In more medieval times, we see love affairs between British King Edward II and his lover Piers Gaveston. We see French King Philip II (Augustus) and his love for Richard the Lionheart. One of the most famous sculptures of all time was Michelangelo's statue of David. The bisexual Michelangelo created a monument to bisexuality in form of the perfect male figure of David for both men and women to behold and to enjoy. The symbolism is profound and rich and need not be seen as dirty or perverted. The statue of David stands as a glorious celebration of 5,000 years of bisexual beauty and exploration.

NOTES

1. Olivia Laing, *The Trip to Echo Spring: On Writers and Drinking*, 2014.
2. C. Reback and S. Larkins, "HIV Risk Behaviors Among a Sample of Heterosexually Identified Men Who Occasionally Have Sex with Another Mane and/or a Transwoman," *Journal of Sex Research* 50, no. 2 (2013): 151–63.
3. Rebak, Larkins, op. cit.
4. Ibid.
5. Ibid.
6. Ibid.
7. Ibid.
8. M. Carrier, "Mexican Male Sexuality," *Journal of Homosexuality* 11, no 1–2 (1985): 75–86.
9. G. Brahmam, V. Kodavella, H. Rajkumar, e H. K. Rachakulla, S. Kallam, S. P. Myakala, R. S. Paranjape, M. D. Gupte, L. Ramakrishnan, A. Kohli, and B. M. Ramesh, "Sexual Practices, HIV and Sexually Transmitted Infections Among Self-Identified Men Who Have Sex with Men in Four High HIV Prevalence States in India," *AIDS* 22 (December 2008): 45–57.
10. "Stigma towards PLWHA: The Role of Internalized Homosexual Stigma in Latino Gay/Bisexual Male and Transgender Communities," *AIDS Education and Prevention* 25, no. 3 (2013): 179–89. Online publication date: June 1, 2013.
11. Brahmam, Ginnela, Kodavalla, et al., "Sexual Practices, HIV and Sexually Transmitted."
12. Reback and Larkins, "HIV Risk Behaviors Among a Sample of Heterosexually Identified Men."
13. S. T. Russell, T. J. Clarke, and J. Clary, "Are Teens 'Post-Gay'? Contemporary Adolescents' Sexual Identity Labels," *Journal of Youth and Adolescence* 38, no. 7 (August 2009): 884–90.
14. M. Bloor, N. McKeganey, and M Bernard, "An Ethnographic Study of HIV-Related Risk Practices Among Glasgow Rent Boys and Their Clients: Report of a Pilot Study," *AIDS Care: Psychological and Socio-medical Aspects of AIDS/HIV* 2, no 1 (Sept. 2007): 17–24; published online September 25, 2007.
15. V. Minichiello,R. Mariño1, J. Browne, M. Jamieson, K. Peterson, B. Reuter, and K. Robinson, "A Profile of the Clients of Male Sex Workers in Three Australian Cities," *Australian and New Zealand Journal of Public Health* 23, no 5 (Oct. 1999): 511–18; article first published online: May 13, 2008.
16. S. Shoptaw, R. Weiss, B. Munjas, C. Hucks-Ortiz, S. Young, S. Larkins, G. Victorianne, and P. Gorbach, "Homonegativity, Substance Use, Sexual Risk Behaviors, and HIV Status in Poor and Ethnic Men Who Have Sex with Men in Los Angeles," *Journal of Urban Health* 86, suppl. 1 (July 2009): 77.
17. C. J. Boyd, S. E. McCabe, and H. d'Arcy, "Ecstasy Use Among College Undergraduates: Gender, Race and Sexual Identity," *Journal of Substance Abuse Treatment* 24, no. 3 (April 2003): 209–15.

18. M. King, J. Semlyen, S. S. Tai, H. Killaspy, D. Osborn, and D. Popelyk, "A Systematic Review of Mental Disorder, Suicide, and Deliberate Self-Harm in Lesbian, Gay and Bisexual People," *BMC Psychiatry* 8, no. 1 (2008): 70.

19. B. Denizet-Lewis, "The Scientific Quest to Prove Bisexuality," *New York Times,* March 20, 2104.

20. A. P. Buxton, "Writing Our Own Script: How Bisexual Men and Their Heterosexual Wives Maintain Their Marriages After Disclosure," *Journal of Bisexuality* 1, (2–3): 155–89. Published online: October 22, 2008.

21. E. Coleman, "Bisexual and Gay Men in Heterosexual Marriage: Conflicts and Resolutions in Therapy," *Journal of Homosexuality* 7, no. 2–3 (1982): 93–103.

22. W. L. Jeffriesa, B. Dodgeb, and T. G. M. Sandfort, "Religion and Spirituality Among Bisexual Black Men in the USA," *Culture, Health & Sexuality: An International Journal for Research, Intervention and Care* 10, no. 5 (2008): 463–47; published online June 17, 2008.

23. N. Nodin, P. Valera, A. Ventuneac, E. Maynard, and A. Carballo-Diéguez, "The Internet Profiles of Men Who Have Sex with Men Within Bareback Websites," *Culture, Health & Sexuality* 13, no. 9 (2011): 1015–29; online publication date August 5, 2011.

24. C. M. Klaar, "Straight Wives of HIV-Positive Husbands Who Contracted the Virus Through Male-to-Male Sexual Contact," *Journal of GLBT Family Studies* 8, no 1 (2012): 99–120; published online January 20, 2012.

Chapter Four

Childhood Sexual Abuse

Tragically Common for Gay Men

ADOLESCENT SEXUAL ABUSE AND RECOVERY

Sexual abuse is one of society's most sensitive "hot button" issues. First, the sexual abuse of a child arouses one-sided emotions, such as universal disgust and the desire to seek retribution, revenge, and punishment—even murder. No one with any shred of moral integrity could possibly support it. Second, conviction of this offense carries the potential lifelong curse of being labeled a "sex offender" in the United States. Third, society strangely treats this issue as if it were a rare occurrence when, sadly, it is appallingly common. This is not a new phenomenon either. More than 120 years ago, Sigmund Freud had a hard time believing just how many girls and boys experienced unwanted sexual encounters from, say, the age of five to fourteen. Fourth, in a world that seems to count everything to the last scintilla, few in the scientific community can agree on even a narrow range when it comes to the percentage of children who have endured sexual abuse.

It is as if we as a society want to stay in denial that our children are being hurt in this way. There seems to be a sense of "if we avoid it, it goes away." For a mother to admit that her child was abused by her husband or by one of her other children is to stab at the heart of the maternal instinct. There is a lot to lose if the event becomes public. Indeed, for too many, especially those in recovery from drug and alcohol addiction, the issue is too hot to handle.

It is my experience that, in the world of drug rehab programs, the number of people who struggle with ongoing trauma stemming from child sexual abuse is staggeringly high. Let's go back to chapter 2, for instance, and consider how many bisexual individuals on the "down-low" were drug users. Of the men in the study who were bisexual addicts, *one in three* reported having experienced unwanted and unsolicited sex at an early age. One of them even admitted being sexually abused by a transgender nanny when he was fourteen years old.

Such experiences leave an indelible mark on a child or young person, one that is not easy to resolve. Without intensive therapy or counseling by trained professionals at some point, the victim may continue to struggle with the effects of abuse in multiple ways for many, many years, and this may manifest in various ways. For example, as adults, victims of abuse may unconsciously try to re-create the feelings associated with their early sexual abuse (including pain, shame, humiliation, powerlessness, and the fear of being caught) in sexual relationships with other adults. This behavior may be related to having a distorted vision of sex, seeing it as an activity surrounded by malfeasance, secrets, negative consequences, and anxiety. In these instances, early sexual abuse seems to form a sexual script—a narrative of forbidden pleasure—and influences the victim's sexual life in adulthood. A central part of this script involves alcohol and drug abuse, which acts as an anesthetic for the emotional wounds caused by acts of betrayal.

All too often, drug rehab counselors—as well as parents, friends, and those trudging the road of recovery themselves—are at a loss for how to help the recovering addict who is an adult survivor of sexual abuse. Of course, there is the issue of which to treat first—the addiction or the underlying trauma. Or, should both be treated simultaneously? For recovery from drug addiction to have any "sticking power," the experience of abuse cannot be swept under the rug. As entwined as the effects of abuse may be with drug abuse, it is essential to uncover these roots and work to resolve them. This will finally allow the person to engage with recovery and move on with life.

This chapter is intended to remove the stigma of sexual abuse and to present it less as a savage rare occurrence and more as an issue akin to teenage obesity or diabetes. Indeed, we will see that it is at least as common as these problems and yet is treated as a rare occurrence and something from which it is difficult if not impossible to gain any emotional freedom in sobriety.

We will also explore how the wisdom growing out of a similar issue in society—soldiers returning from battle with PTSD—can be applied to the world of healing from sexual abuse. PTSD is all too common in military veterans and now, after being in denial about this sensitive issue for many years, society as a whole is rolling up its sleeves and creating solutions for this scourge affecting hundreds of thousands of Americans.

Although gay men in recovery have not faced the hazards of battle as brave soldiers have done, they have been surrounded by a slew of other life-threatening events—deaths of friends from AIDS/HIV, bullying and beatings from an early age, overt discrimination, physical consequences from reckless drug taking, and frequent experiences of childhood sexual abuse and/or rape.

THE PROFILE OF THOSE WHO ARE ABUSING

Who is sexually abusing children and young adolescents? The span of adult abusers of children goes wide and far. A significant majority of sexual abuse comes from family members or family friends. While some young people are abused by strangers, this occurs only in a small minority of instances. One-third of sexual abusers are juveniles.[1] Underage kids also sexually abuse other younger children. There are also many cases of underage teens being indicted for abusive behavior in the form of "sexting"—for instance, a betrayal involving one underage sex partner who forwards nude images of another underage partner to other students in the high school. Is this a crime, and, if so, does this person deserve to be branded a "sex offender"? This is a new realm of illegal activity with which law enforcement in the United States is currently grappling. In addition, there are cases of teens which concoct malicious stories in order to extort money from adults, especially in the gay world. Separating the true from the false is also a problem in the counting of what is "abuse."

Note

1. David Finkelhor, "The Prevention of Childhood Sexual Abuse," *The Future of Children* 19, no. 2 (Fall 2009): 169–94.

DIAGNOSIS OF THE PUBLIC HEALTH CRISIS OF SEXUAL ABUSE

Before we try to unwind and consider how to alter this tragic and repetitive script of sexual dysfunctionality due to childhood sexual abuse, let's quantify the problem in the population as a whole. Then, we will try to determine the degree to which this is magnified within the population of gay and bisexual men who are seeking recovery for addiction. As we do this, bear in mind a few important data points. First, gay men are three to four times more likely to experience problems with substance abuse.[1] And, as we saw earlier, bisexual teens had problems with substance abuse even more than gay men; accurate numbers for adult bisexual men who abuse substances are hard to come by. Furthermore, we will see how common a history of childhood sexual abuse is for gay men in recovery. So, this chapter is highly relevant to the recovery process for gay men (and bisexual men as well as lesbians) who are addicts. I personally see this issue as one of the last remaining "elephant in the living room" in the treatment for addiction.

One of the more comprehensive studies on sexual abuse was completed in 2007 by the renowned David Finkelhor of the University of New Hampshire. In his meta-analysis, Finkelhor reviewed sixty-five articles from twenty-two countries and found that 8 percent of men and 20 percent of women had suffered some form of unwanted sexual encounter prior to age eighteen.[2] Another study suggested that between 15 and 25 percent of girls in the United States are sexually abused at some point before adulthood.[3] As we'll discuss more in a bit, these numbers exceed that of youths who experience either teenage diabetes or obesity.

Another peer-reviewed study found evidence of much higher rates of sexual abuse rates among gays and lesbians.[4] And a separate large-scale study of more than 15,000 gay men concluded that 27 percent were sexually abused in childhood. Furthermore, this study showed that gay men who were sexually abused were more likely to be HIV-positive—because these men also reported frequent casual male partners, substance use, and unprotected sex while under the influence of alcohol or other drugs. Were they living out a sexual script of self-loathing, self-destruction, and anxiety? It seems so.[5] Like other studies on this subject, this report stressed that "inconsistencies across studies indicated a need to reach consensus among researchers and providers in defining childhood sexual abuse."

A prime example of the extreme inconsistencies in research findings—and, some would argue, a wildly inaccurate range of data—comes from one of the most comprehensive meta-analyses and involved 166 studies, probably one of the largest analyses of its kind ever. The conclusions of this report, published in the prestigious *Journal of the American Medical Association,* included several shocking statistics: First, the estimated prevalence of sexual abuse of boys in the United States varied widely (by definition used and population studied), ranging from 4 to 76 percent. Second, boys under the age of twelve living in poor socioeconomic conditions were most at risk. Perpetrators tended to be known but unrelated males. Abuse frequently occurred outside the home, involved penetration, and occurred more than once. Third, adult outcomes included psychological distress, substance abuse, and sexually related problems.[6] We will see this phrasing over and over again. It is a sad refrain for those victims who are locked into a tragic narrative of depression, anxiety, low self-esteem, and stress. Lastly, two important studies reinforced the pervasiveness of childhood sexual abuse. In a large meta-study, researchers made the staggering claim that 30–40 percent of girls and 13 percent of boys had been sexually abused as children.[7]

And a controversial study by the University of Southern California concluded that, in the group of men and women they surveyed, 14 percent of the men and 32 percent of the women reported childhood experiences that would be considered sexual abuse.[8] This study was controversial because it stated loud and clear that "childhood sexual and physical abuse is relatively common in the general population."

Furthermore, the study found that adolescents who had experienced sexual abuse met ten of ten of the criteria for the Trauma Symptom Inventory (TSI), a measure of post-traumatic distress disorder (PTSD). If there is a high rate of childhood sexual abuse among gay, lesbian, and bisexuals in recovery, then we also need to assume that a large proportion of this group (possibly as many as one in three) likely suffer from some form of PTSD. We will pick up this thread in a later section, but this startling data point underlies much of this chapter.

These many references to research studies tell us much about the incidence of childhood sexual abuse. First, the abuse is significant, with averages for boys falling into the 14–18 percent range and girls falling into the 20–25 percent range (with an admittedly large standard deviation). Second, it is likely under-reported for various reasons, including shame and fear of consequences to the abuser. Third, the reported prevalence varies wildly depending on how we define abuse; in all, the number of boys who experienced sexual abuse ranged from 4 to 76 percent and the range of girls being sexually abused was reported anywhere from 15 to 40 percent. Fourth, a history of childhood sexual abuse appears to be significantly higher for gay and lesbians who are in recovery for drug and alcohol abuse. My own experience in talking with hundreds of gays and lesbians over the past decade is that about one-third of men in recovery have had some form of unwanted sexual encounter, and more than 40 percent of women in recovery experienced unwanted sexual encounters as children. Fifth, a significant swing factor for people in recovery is the way that they deal with this painful secret. Sixth, a vitally important discovery, which is a key theme in this chapter, is that gay and bisexual men who are in recovery for drug addiction and who have been victims of unwanted sexual encounters in their youth have symptoms of PTSD. This is often unrecognized in recovery circles.

Further, there is widespread agreement in addiction circles that childhood sexual trauma plays a large part in the development of addiction. Therefore, it should play a large role in the way out of addiction. It is my experience that those who can admit the abused occurred, talk about it, and find some sort of forgiveness for the perpetrator have a far better chance of sustained and continuous recovery.

Those who do not will tend to relapse as they live in a world of rage, victimization, and self-loathing. This is, I believe, a kind of self-constructed trap. Addiction needs victimization to work. Victims have someone to "drink at." They feel entitled to harm themselves (with cutting, drugs, unsafe sex, binge eating, etc.) because they have been wronged. The feeling of being a victim and being wrong creates that isolation so essential for the addictive process to take over.

HIV AND GAY MEN: WE MUST ADDRESS MENTAL ISSUES AND SUBSTANCE ABUSE OR HIV RATES MAY NOT FALL

One of the unintended consequences of the HIV/AIDS epidemic has been the ability to gain immense amounts of information about gay men that were never available before. Gay men have a much higher frequency of partner violence, depression, childhood sexual trauma, and substance abuse than the general population. Furthermore, these health conditions seem to be independent of each other. The highest correlated set of events was between childhood sexual abuse and poly-drug use. In other words, gay men who were sexually abused have a very decent chance of becoming a poly drug user.

The question asked by Ron Stall and his colleagues at the CDC in Atlanta is what combinations of past events or conditions are most likely to lead to HIV infection? This is important in arriving at ways to prevent HIV infection. If all of these types of past conditions—depression, sexual abuse, drug use, or partner violence—seem to be a set of random events when it comes to determining which of these events leads to HIV infection, it is hard to know what to address in order to prevent HIV.

The disturbing conclusions of this study were that there is an interplay of these health problems which *magnifies* the vulnerability of a population to HIV. By themselves, physical abuse, sexual abuse as a child, substance abuse, or depression do not seem to lead to HIV infection. Together, they produce a toxic cocktail which has a high chance of bringing on HIV infection. In other words, events such as depression, sexual abuse, substance abuse, and partner violence are not additive. They are geometric and lead to dramatically higher rates of HIV infection when brought together in one person. The more a gay man has to cope with a number of life issues such as depression, spousal abuse, or substance abuse, the more likely he is to contract HIV. A population suffering from this syndemic of multiple factors leads to high rates of HIV infection. Other subgroups which are at especially high risk include gay American Indians and gay African Americans. An important conclusion here is that fighting HIV infection means attacking several prior psychosocial issues for both white and minority gay men. Mental health needs to be addressed. The other issue which needs to be addressed is spousal violence. And issues of substance abuse must be addressed. Without addressing substance abuse and mental issues, it is unlikely that HIV rates will drop.

The bottom line? "Men who are mired in the combined effects of substance abuse, depression, violence and painful memories of past sexual abuse may not have the capacity to reduce their sexual risk."[1] Recommendations include: (1) HIV prevention programs need to partner with mental health and substance abuse programs to have any real effect. MSM are usually battling multiple mental health issues, so the response to reduce HIV infection must be done on multiple fronts within the community. (2) Lifelong effects of marginalization and stigmatization often create these psychosocial problems. Stress, anxiety, homophobia and workforce issues add to these problems. How can these factors that create syndemics be disrupted?

Note

1. Ron Stall, Thomas Mills, John Williamson, et al. Association of Co-Occurring Psychosocial Health Problems and Increased Vulnerability to HIV/AIDS Among Urban Men Who Have Sex with Men," *American Journal of Public Health*, Vol. 93, No. 6. June 2003.

This isolation creates fear and rage, a feeling of being trapped. The person feels pushed into a corner and isolated. He or she is all alone. This sense of eroticized fear can lead to anonymous sexual encounters with strangers which perversely reinforces fear, since the sexual acting out exposes a person to risk of arrest or expulsion from the group. Eroticized rage can lead to sexual acting out which suggests punishment. The person may feel he or she needs to be punished in the act of sex, so may be bug chasers. They will seek out STDs or may want to be "bred," i.e. they will want someone to infect them in a highly eroticized act of spreading HIV. This can explain why those who have experienced sexual of physical abuse have higher incidents of HIV transmission than those who did not experience sexual or physical abuse. This hamster wheel of shame, self-loathing, sickness, seeking out sickness—and then experiencing more shame—can only be broken by making a break with an abusive past. It is my experience that some form of reconciliation or forgiveness must occur for this cycle to stop. In this way, the Twelve Step programs offer a way out, since Steps Eight and Nine are all about seeking forgiveness and forgiving. I have always thought that, in this issue, forgiveness of the self is almost more important than forgiveness for the perpetrator. The act of the abuse suggests a deep sense of powerlessness over life (why could I not stop it and why wasn't someone watching over me?) that causes one to conclude that life is a random set of unfortunate events from which it is impossible to escape. This creates a sense of cynicism, negativity, and despair which makes alcohol and drugs seem attractive. Twelve Step programs have an answer to this. We are all precisely powerless over the violence which life throws at us, but there is a higher power that can offer hope and a way out in times of despair. In Twelve Step parlance, there is a helpful phrase, "I am powerless, but I am not helpless!"

This reconciliation can go a long way to reconciling the good side with the "bad" or "evil " side where one can bring together a past where sexual encounters occurred which were unwanted. Finding some pity for the perpetrator is a viable way out, indeed. It can go a long way toward creating a united self and allow a person to stand up tall. It is a matter of saying, "I did not cause it. I did not start it. I do not excuse the behavior. I forgive the behavior." In this step is a way out of the self-harm and self-abuse. Thousands of years of human healing strongly suggest that forgiveness of the self and the perpetrator is a powerful and life-giving way out of the morass and self-reinforcing destruction of all that is worthwhile when one is going down the drain from substance abuse driven by being a victim. One powerful phrase I heard in one group session I helped coordinate came from someone who was also in a Twelve Step program, He said, "The Twelve Steps of AA helped me to let myself off the hook for being a victim all my life."

PREVENTION OF SEXUAL ABUSE AMONG YOUTH

There are two elements of this chronic mental health issue that need to be laid out. The first is about the importance of initiating a healthy public discussion to address the current generation of youth who are at risk for unwanted sexual encounters. This is the issue of prevention. In this discussion, we'll consider two examples of serious public health issues involving teenagers that are now receiving much attention but were given short shrift only a few years ago. One is teenage obesity, which is reported to afflict about 11 to 15 percent of the teen population. Another is teenage diabetes, which afflicts a similar proportion of the population. If the studies discussed above are correct, childhood sexual abuse would be in a range similar to both adolescent diabetes and obesity.

Though child sexual abuse and teen obesity as well as teen diabetes affect roughly the same percentage of the population, today we see a proliferation of information and publicity about the nutrition and sugar reduction but little on the sexual abuse. For example, there are obesity and diabetes pamphlets, education programs, ad campaigns, presidential support programs, national funding, grants, university programs, and so forth, but few high profile state or federal programs aimed at reducing or eliminating childhood sexual abuse. Nor is there much in the way of focused public attention, funding, advertising, national campaigns, or university support for the thorny and hypersensitive issue of sexual abuse.

Sexual abuse is something that is still in the closet or swept under the carpet. It is seen as too hot to handle. This is supremely ironic because this form of abuse is so common and leads to significant mental health problems that cost billions of dollars for adults who flounder in shame, anxiety, drug addiction, and loneliness due to a lack of resources. This includes billions of dollars in lost work, mental health problems, physical ailments, suicidality, criminality, and a tragic cycle of sexual crimes.

If adolescent obesity or diabetes affects about 11 to 15 percent of adolescents, and *at least* 10 percent of adolescents have had an unwanted sexual encounter, isn't it time to stop thinking that sexual abuse does not exist or, worse, that it is some extremely rare taboo subject? This attitude keeps an odor of stigma around the subject and prevents a solid, calm, and focused public response both from general helping professionals and from recovery treatment providers.

An attitude of "This could never happen in my home" is simply not good enough, nor is it accurate. The numbers laid out above strongly suggest that we should actually be starting with the issue of childhood sexual abuse when dealing with underlying trauma for men and women in recovery for substance abuse. This is bound, in my opinion, to capture at least one-third of a recovery group.

The proportion of childhood sexual abuse among people in treatment for drug and alcohol abuse is exceptionally high, and yet few rehab programs have explicit programs to deal with this problem. What's more, in addiction circles, sexual abuse is rarely considered when diagnosing underlying conditions of the addiction and subsequent treatment plans, including treatment for PTSD. This, even though it is all too clear among people in the addiction field that childhood sexual abuse often plays a key role in the pathology of addiction. Further, in a world where addicts often have tawdry, ghastly, or astonishing "drunk-alogues," the issue of sexual abuse is, in my experience, treated as an uncomfortable topic that should be saved "for another time."

Greater openness is required to tackle the uncomfortable and thorny topic of unwanted sexual encounters for teenagers and younger children. In the case of teen diabetes or obesity, we may experience some discomfort about the topic but there is no one to arrest for the condition, no "predator" who is knowingly performing illegal activity. (Although some health activists are seeking to treat cereal companies who add copious amounts of sugar to their products as "predators" as well.) In addition, diabetes and obesity may have genetic characteristics, which hamper the discussion of accountability. So, they remain medical problems and not moral issues. (On a "morally neutral" issue like this, it is remarkable how much pushback and protest there was when Mayor Bloomberg of New York tried to make this issue front and center and reduce sugar intake. His suggestions were taken as an outrageous assault on individual liberty.)

The issues are far more profound in the case of adults who are making sexual advances on minors. These people can be arrested and face serious, lifelong consequences. Furthermore, families are often torn apart when one of the members is responsible and the judicial system becomes involved. While obesity and diabetes may put a strain on a family, sexual abuse can easily rip apart and destroy a family unit. And those who were not responsible can carry great enduring guilt and shame for "not preventing" the assault.

Furthermore, issues of obesity and diabetes are now commonly discussed issues and parents everywhere are taking matters into their own hands and following simple recommendations from an assortment of professional associations formed to deal with these very serious health issues. They are no longer embarrassing subjects that need to be swept under the carpet or ignored—or, worse, laughed at. We need to take steps to change the prevailing view of childhood sexual abuse. No longer can the very subject be considered taboo; it needs to be discussed in the same open and forthright way that teen obesity or diabetes is today. This will open the door to real progress.

TREATMENT FOR ADULT VICTIMS OF SEXUAL ABUSE

The other element of childhood sexual abuse that merits discussion is treatment and the important issue of healing adults who have survived such abuse and want to move on with their lives. All too often, they are stuck in an unhealthy narrative in which they see themselves as victims and so create "self-sabotage" circumstances where they trap themselves in abusive relationships and do not see a way out. This is especially important to those gay, bisexual, and lesbian men and women who are in recovery from drug and alcohol abuse. Toward this end, we need to address the following issues:

1. A widespread problem. The first message that we need to convey to victims is that these experiences are astoundingly common, as the previous section noted. They seem to be a disturbingly common feature of human nature. Carl Jung discussed this dark predilection of human nature in some controversial writings.[9] The commonness does not reduce the pain, but it does allow more people to come forward and talk about events that they "swore they would take to their grave."
2. Self-blame. For the gay or bisexual man, the issue of sexual abuse is one of deep conflict: On the one hand, it was an event when an adult took unfair advantage of a boy or young teenager who did not know better and lacked the judgment or physical/mental strength to resist the encounter. On the other hand, there is very often guilt that "they liked it" and often

"went back for more." Repeated encounters created a relationship of sorts and when this relationship is suddenly "broken apart" or "abruptly stopped" because of the discovery by a parent or another adult, a series of unintended consequences can ensue. Separating the event from the victim is important. There is a need to escape a lifetime script of "being a victim"; that is, of being trapped in a broken record of playing the role of a victim.

3. The non-family abuser. Let's take the case of a non-family abuser. When there is an intervention of some sort by parents or police and the abuser is removed from the scene, this is undoubtedly a worthy outcome. The adolescent is saved from further harm. And if the abuser had threatened physical violence toward the adolescent in the event of disclosure, it is ideal for separation and arrest to take place. If, however, the adolescent and adult abuser had formed a kind of relationship and then the adult suddenly disappears without explanation (since parents or guardians are loathe to discuss such a sensitive subject even with their own child), the adolescent is left wondering what happened.

   Ironically, this may leave the youth with a sense of abandonment. "Why did this person who showed interest in me suddenly leave?" Another feeling often emerges as well—one of guilt. As someone who "went back for more sex with a man because he liked it," this adolescent may feel responsible for the adult's removal from the community or worse. Such feelings of abandonment or guilt among sexually abused children are mentioned frequently in literature on this subject.

4. Immediate therapy. My own experience in working with survivors of adolescent sexual abuse is that we have a golden opportunity to prevent a great deal of adult problems with sexuality if the parents or guardians—in alliance with a competent psychologist—have family therapy sessions immediately and engage in what need to be adult conversations about what the boy or girl feels at the moment. It is critical that feelings of guilt or shame or abandonment—among a number of other emotions—are fully explored. Parents should rally behind their child and reassure him or her of their love. Parents could allow one hour per week to let their child vent emotions and reflect on what happened until there is little more to discuss. This may be a few sessions or many.

5. Family member. When the sexual abuser is a sibling or other close relative within the nuclear family, the required response is very different—and more complex—than if the abuser was a stranger or a neighbor. The stakes are very high here. How the abuse is handled may have significant consequences for the victim and for the family as a whole. With a stranger, it is possible (indeed, desirable) to put the person in jail or otherwise find a way to banish him or her from the family. But is it possible for a family

to rally around one member (the abused) and put the other member (the abuser) in jail and then just continue on with life? Can they expel or banish the abuser from the family entirely? Does the family unit have any responsibility to address the person's possible substance abuse or previous sexual abuse experiences, which led him down this terrible road? When the abuse occurred between their own children (or with their children or older relatives), the parents always risks destroying at least one life in their response. If the abuser is arrested, the victim is also exposed as the craven child who was, some might whisper, just a little too curious for his or her own good. In most cases, the rumors will abound.

Again, abused adolescents may feel that they have done something terrible since the person with whom they have been intimate has been banished or arrested. They may wrongly feel responsible for the abuse, even though it is the adult who should have known better and who must pay the consequences for choices made. The starting point, therefore, should be to quickly address the situation and let the adolescent that he or she did nothing wrong. He or she is a minor and has not developed full judgment. It's important that the first response from the parent or guardian be one of support and love.

It is especially important to tell boys that same-sex interest is common in early adolescence between the ages of about eleven and fourteen.[10] The numbers vary, but as many as 40 percent of adolescent boys have had a sexual encounter with another boy. This is a natural curiosity and a somewhat common phase that most boys outgrow as they mature and subsequently become attracted to girls. Having had a "gay" encounter with another boy does not make someone gay. There is nothing wrong with this and pointing out the prevalence of such behavior is both accurate and appropriate.

Conversely, it is important to point out that there is no reason to paint the abuser as a gay person. In one study, 82 percent of sexual abuse cases involved an alleged offender who was a heterosexual family member or other close relative of the child.[11] The discussion and counseling by family members do not need to go down the road of recrimination and self-condemnation. Anger and rage may initially drive the emotional train, but love, tolerance, and forgiveness should drive the process of healing. This is ideal that is not often achieved, but it truly is the best outcome for a gay, bisexual, or lesbian in recovery who wants to overcome lifelong feelings of shame, self-disgust, and sexual dysfunction.

6. A family affair. My experience is that it can be very healing for the entire family to gather around the table and have a frank dialogue about the incident. This can be done in a calm and loving environment that does not

assign blame but rather strives to create healing from a devastating incident. In any event, people talk. A significant happening between two members of a family unit cannot be kept a secret forever. Having this "secret" hover around creates the infamous "elephant in the living room." It grows into an unnecessary monster and creates a dysfunctional unit. Talk therapy is always better than badly kept secrets.

JACK'S STORY

Jack is a thirty-nine-year old man who has been sober two years. In early sobriety, he used the Twelve Step program of Alcoholics Anonymous, as well as a professional therapist, to confront a deep secret: When he was thirteen, he had multiple sexual encounters with his nineteen-year-old brother. At the time, he had great shame and guilt about the encounters. He knew the activity was wrong because it was "gay" and because it was with a sibling. Gay incest was the worst thing ever, wasn't it? After several encounters, his brother suddenly disappeared—he up and moved halfway across the country and afterward no one in his family ever talked about why he left. In fact, they never really discussed him at all. Jack knew in his heart that something had gone horribly wrong and he privately felt responsible even though his family was acting in his best interests. Instead, Jack thought he was responsible for ruining his brother's life.

He buried the secret of their sexual encounters for many years, never even suggesting the subject in discussions with his parents or his other three siblings. Everyone just seemed to block it and his brother's very existence out. For many years, Jack privately questioned whether he had "caused" his brother's banishment or if he was to blame for the great rift he felt in his family. He also felt abandoned by his brother because, after the first incident of abuse, he had actually gone back for more sex—he "liked" it. Even though he was much younger and did not know better—and his older brother should have known better—these facts did not help him during those many years of conflicted feelings. Indeed, he struggled with (1) shame for liking it; (2) abandonment that his brother had disappeared so quickly; (3) guilt for feeling partly responsible for his brother's banishment; (4) fear and self-disgust that this sexual activity "marked" him as gay; and (5) a sense of doom that he would never be "normal" again after being involved in "gay incest." As an adult, Jack carried on with what many call the "script" of the sexually abused. It wasn't until he became sober and entered recovery and started therapy that he learned that having a few sexual liaisons with his brother when he was thirteen did *not* make him gay.

TAKING THE RATTLING BOX DOWN FROM THE ATTIC

Jack's story resembles that of many adults who have found peace and grounding (and continuous sobriety) when they confront the scary issue of sexual abuse. Many people like Jack say, "By the time I had my first drink, I needed it." Jack eventually learned in therapy and early sobriety that the way his family had handled the situation was hardly ideal. He also learned that there was *a lot* more sexual abuse occurring in his family than he ever realized. He found out later still, when he forgave his older brother, that this brother was himself sexually abused when he was ten and that he had been addicted to cocaine at the time when he began to sexually abuse Jack. In therapy, Jack also learned that it was normal to feel abandonment and guilt in his circumstances, especially when the perpetrator is abruptly taken out of the picture and the victim does not receive any counseling. And the hardest thing to swallow for Jack was, as an adult man, admitting out loud that he went back for more and he liked it. It was not the act itself which caused the shame—the shame came from the fact that he liked it. This revelation was important for Jack in that it help to ameliorate his shame. The brother was absolutely wrong for abusing Jack, but Jack had a part in it as well. This made it easier for him to forgive his brother without excusing the unacceptable behavior.

Many gay men are at a loss about how to pick up the issue of sexual abuse and explore it to another adult they can trust to help them process the event and find some resolution. So they simply set the issue of sexual abuse aside but it does not die; instead it becomes a "rattling box" in the attic that is too dangerous to bring down to the living room and open. It is simply too hot to handle because it involves a wound (trauma is Greek for "wound") to a child and now their adult self must help the child within heal. This is simply too difficult for many adults, so they turn to alcohol and drugs to drown out the rattling noises in the attic. How on earth can the healing process start except by getting help to go into the attic of the psyche, bring down the rattling box marked "abuse," and open it up in a protected environment with safe and competent adults? Perhaps we can get some glimpses about how adults can deal with this trauma by looking at the advice given to teens about the issue.

If 10 percent of adults in the United States have issues with substance abuse, and if 10 percent of these adults are struggling with memories of an unwanted sexual encounter, that makes about 1.5 million American adults who may need help in dealing with an issue that they often think happened to no one else and that is a permanent open sore for which there is no tonic or relief. Drugs and alcohol seem to be the only way to keep the pain at bay. What's more, they are often caught in the sexual narrative that sex needs to be dangerous, illicit, forbidden, and painful because that was how they first experienced it.

Of the approximately 1.5 million Americans looking for some relief from adult mental health issues related to unwanted adolescent sexual encounters, hundreds of thousands of these people are also addicts. To meet that significant demand for help we have 130,000 members of the American Psychological Association and about 36,000 members of the American Psychiatric Association. When you also consider the host of other mental health issues out there, it's clear that there is a severe deficit of resources available for this widespread mental health issue.

People who suffer from sexual abuse often seek out help through a) group therapy; b) Twelve Step programs for substance abuse or sexual acting out; c) community programs for healing from abuse; d) spirituality; e) family members who are safe and responsible to talk to; and f) self-help measures like meditation and exercise. Service-oriented activity to help others, especially victims of abuse who are suffering, is an age-old way to heal. An example of this is to receive training for suicide hotlines.

There are many programs but few of them are fully equipped to deal with this issue and progress is impeded. This is because sexual abuse has such a powerful stigma that society seems to think it is some incurable and rare 'sickness.' In fact it is more common than teen obesity or teen diabetes, so there should be a floodgate of activity to deal with the issue. This issue is very similar to another former "elephant in the living room" and that is post-traumatic stress disorder in wounded warriors returning from battle in the Middle East. That, too, once carried a stigma that impeded societal responses which are mature, forthright, sturdy, and organized.

NOTES

1. Alan Downs, *The Velvet Rage: Overcoming the Pain of Growing Up Gay in a Straight Man's World,* second edition (New York: DeCapo, 2012), 142.
2. Noemí Peredaa, Georgina Guilerab, Maria Fornsa, and Juana Gómez-Benitob, "The Prevalence of Child Sexual Abuse in Community and Student Samples: A Meta-analysis," *Clinical Psychology Review* 29, no. 4 (June 2009): 328–38.
3. Jane Leserman, "Sexual Abuse History: Prevalence, Health Effects, Mediators, and Psychological Treatment," *Psychosomatic Medicine* 67, no. 6 (November/December 2005): 906–15.
4. Elizabeth Saewyc, Carol Skay, Kimberly Richens, Elizabeth Reis, Colleen Poon, and Aileen Murphy, "Sexual Orientation, Sexual Abuse, and HIV-Risk Behaviors Among Adolescents in the Pacific Northwest," *American Journal of Public Health* 96, no. 6 (June 2006): 1104–10.

5. Shane Lloyd and Don Operario, "HIV Risk Among Men Who Have Sex with Men Who Have Experienced Childhood Sexual Abuse: Systematic Review and Meta-Analysis," *AIDS Education and Prevention* 24, no. 3 (2012): 228–41.

6. William C. Holmes and Gail B. Slap, "Sexual Abuse of Boys: Definition, Prevalence, Correlates, Sequelae, and Management," *Journal of the American Medical Association* 280, no. 21 (1998): 1855–62.

7. Rebecca M. Bolen and Maria Scannapieco, "Prevalence of Child Sexual Abuse: A Corrective Meta-analysis," *Social Service Review* (73, no. 3 (1999): 281.

8. John Briere and Diana M. Elliott, "Prevalence and Psychological Sequelae of Self-Reported Childhood Physical and Sexual Abuse in a General Population Sample of Men and Women," *Child Abuse and Neglect* 27, no. 10 (October 2003): 1205–22.

9. Carl Jung discussed the issues of incest and sexual attraction to young people as part of the shadow—that unconscious part of the person that holds the negative or evil side of us and represents primitive and uncivilized elements, which are often seen as repugnant. Though generally repressed, this part of the person needs to be recognized in a way that does not challenge the positive view of a person he or she wishes to represent to the world. This is reflective of William James's idea that the key to forgiveness is seeing how we are all capable of evil and all of us—doctors and lunatics—"come from the same clay." The precise quotation is as follows: "Whenever [the] drive for wholeness appears, it begins by disguising itself under the symbolism of incest, for, unless he seeks it in himself, a man's nearest feminine counterpart is to be found in his mother, sister, or daughter." ("The Psychology of the Transference," CW 16, par. 471, http://www.jungny.com/lexicon.jungian.therapy.analysis/carl.jung.102.html.)

10. Gary Remafedi, "Male Homosexuality: The Adolescent's Perspective," *Pediatrics*. 79, no. 3 (March 1, 1987): 326–30.

11. Carole Jenny, Thomas A. Roesler, and Kimberly L. Poyer, "Are Children at Risk for Sexual Abuse by Homosexuals?" *Pediatrics* 94, no. 1 (July 1, 1994): 41–4.

Part Two

BIO-PSYCHO-SOCIAL RECOVERY FOR GAY AND BISEXUAL MEN

Chapter Five

The Biological. PTSD

The Gay Community Can Learn from Veterans

We honor those who have served our country in battle. Members of the armed forces who have looked death in the face, witnessed the death of their comrades, or suffered a severe traumatic event often return home and encounter problems with survivor's guilt. They ask why they survived while others did not. They replay events in their minds and ask, "Was it my fault that events played out that way?" They question themselves and their decisions, and ask if their own "poor judgment" caused their friends to get hurt or die. They obsess over memories and cannot let go of the trauma. They wonder, "What else could I have done?" They have a narrative that continually draws them back into the memories of the risky behavior—or the risky behavior itself.

Humans have an eerie desire to repeat trauma that they cannot resolve. They become "addicted" to risk, danger, and potentially deadly circumstances. Do they secretly harbor a death wish? Do they seek out risk because they want to prove that, in battle, they do have good judgment? Do they put themselves in harm's way because they privately do not think they deserve to live since they did not protect their comrades? Do they long for the danger because at least in that danger they had a camaraderie and a closeness that they cannot find in normal life?

This issue is way beyond the scope of this chapter. The point here is that we are now dealing with such a high number of adult men and women veterans who are suffering from a condition that is overwhelming society. Suicide rates for this population are staggeringly high, with some estimates suggesting that there is one suicide per hour in the United States by a soldier or veteran with PTSD. Compounding their actual disorder, they have an unusually high rate of unemployment; they cannot hold down jobs; and they have high rates of alcoholism and drug abuse. The good news is that, through the work of many active military officers and veterans who have become counselors, we now have an array of interesting and innovative tools to help veterans cope with PTSD in civilian life.

The lives of gay men who have experienced sexual abuse (and/or physical and emotional abuse including beatings, harassment, or exclusion) are, of course, very different from these brave veterans who fought enemy combatants. And yet study after study indicates that children—especially adolescents who are gay or bisexual—who have experienced sexual abuse (and physical abuse) are more prone to substance abuse in adult life as well as a "co-morbidity" of PTSD. We saw earlier that gay men who have experienced sexual abuse are at high risk for substance abuse. In one study, caregivers noted a high incidence of PTSD for survivors of sexual and physical abuse. Boys were more prone to PTSD than girls, and boys who were both physically and sexually abused were more prone to problems with substance abuse. As the study concluded, "Younger onset and coercion to maintain secrecy (during an episode of sexual abuse) predicted a higher number of PTSD diagnoses."[1] Other studies have corroborated a relationship of child sexual abuse with symptoms of PTSD, including anxiety, irrational fear, suicidal ideas, depression, and substance abuse.[2] These are the very same symptoms that many "wounded warriors" deal with.

If we add to this a toxic mix of shame about being gay or bisexual, we can arrive at a pathology that is deeply troubling for the adult gay or bisexual man who may have experienced sexual and/or physical abuse and is seeking recovery for drug addiction. This says nothing of the various forms of bullying, beatings, name-calling, and harassment that some gay people have endured. Just about every adult gay man has a story about being called a "faggot" or "sissy," or about being beat up in school for effeminate or "questionable" behavior. (Chapter 4 will discuss the treatment approach outlined in Alan Downs' s bestselling book *The Velvet Rage* for dealing with the shame and self-loathing in early adolescence that often leads substance abuse for gay men.)

Times are changing, but the pace of change is slow. For instance, it is surprising to see that a survey from the Human Rights Campaign Fund (HRC) concluded that 53 percent of LGBT employees are not "out" at work, and 25 percent of adult gay people report that they continue to hear offensive comments such as "That's so gay." This is a poll from 2013—not 1983. Of those polled, 20 percent said they had actively looked for a new job because their work environment was not accepting. What is surprising is that while 53 percent were not out at work, the number was 51 percent in a similar poll in 2009. Indeed, there is still a high degree of stresses in the adult lives of gay men and women—personally and professionally. This stress accumulates and has considerable consequences.

WHAT CONNECTS THE SOLDIER WITH PTSD TO THE GAY MAN WITH PTSD?

When I was doing my internship in counseling in 2005 and 2006, there were many soldiers returning from Iraq who had PTSD and were also struggling with drug addiction. As I reflect back on the fundamental problem of unresolved grief that is PTSD, I recall so many of these brave men, some weeping uncontrollably, saying one common theme: "I was powerless to help my buddy when he was blown up by an IED. I was powerless to save his life." Is this underlying rage and anguish of PTSD a basic issue of an unwillingness to say how powerless they were in the face of artillery, IEDs, and bullets? In many ways, the underlying start of the addiction is also a realization of powerlessness.

What a soldier misses about war is the elusive brotherhood that tries to overcome the powerlessness of life which goes away when he returns home. What the addict misses about drugs is the elusive connection to some other realm which goes away when the high fades away and the morning hangover is all there is. Brotherhood in violent battle provides a powerful and addictive connection, because it is very hard to repeat this brotherhood in normal life. Courage to protect another in the face of danger is a noble thing and can be transformed into a great asset as veterans help others suffering from PTSD in normal life. This is also the essence of the Twelve Step program: those addicted to the elusive danger and camaraderie to alcohol and drugs can find a new camaraderie in volunteering to help others in the struggle. There is something fundamentally redeeming when someone volunteers to help another tormented soul recover from that which ails that person who is doing the volunteering. The group is put ahead of self and the person doing the volunteering has moments of self-forgetfulness and the aching need to belong to something illusory and dangerous fades away.

Selfless behavior drags a recovering addict away from the danger and emptiness of drugs. Volunteerism for veterans to help others with PTSD seems to drag them away from the panicky and emasculating feelings of helplessness or powerlessness. Veterans' movements like www.soldieron.org.au are a great example for the gay community to emulate as it tries to heal the wounds of those "rainbow warriors" who are the walking wounded with moderate to severe PTSD. Too many gay men have seen too much death, disease, and suffering due to the modern scourge of AIDS-related sicknesses.

Adult men who are gay or bisexual and are dealing with (1) relapse and substance abuse; (2) drug-taking experiences that involve trauma; and (3) childhood sexual abuse and or physical abuse (whether at home or bullying at school) are at high risk for developing PTSD. This is a different form of PTSD than the life-threatening PTSD that brave combat soldiers develop when they see their friends get killed, but similarities certainly exist. Everyone's pain is their own and no matter how traumatic, it looms large within the mind of each individual. The rattling boxes in the attic are scary indeed. Gay and bisexual men often have loud rattling boxes in the attic which are too scary to be retrieved.

The reason I started this chapter with the example of PTSD and the military is because the gay community can learn a lot from what the military are doing to help their wounded warriors to heal and aid those in need of reconciling (whether accurate or not) a tragic array of feelings as they struggle with the following issues:

1. Guilt: Why did I survive the event? What happened to the other guy? Why him and not me?
2. Remorse: Couldn't I have done more to prevent the event? Am I incompetent after all the experience I have?
3. Shame: I ducked and the other guy didn't and now he's dead. What about my other friends who have fallen around me? Is it all just dumb luck?
4. Cowardice: Why didn't I do more to prevent the damage in all of my adult relationships? Am I a coward?

The approach to these painful questions, combined with a toxic blend of emotions they call up, cause deep trauma for veterans. For many of them, it seems as if there is no way out—no consolation, no relief, and no possible future. And yet there is a developing twofold approach to the issue of military PTSD, which is a fascinating model for the treatment community to follow with gays, bisexuals, and lesbians who have experienced sexual abuse. It involves creating mythology: reorienting the narrative by creating distance from the pain in order to change the meaning of the event and create pride in being a survivor (healing the wounded warrior); and it involves brain chemistry, i.e., dealing directly with the brain chemistry in order to moderate extreme emotions.

CREATING A MYTHOLOGY

One very popular approach to creating distance from the pain, regain pride in one's self, and change behavior is to re-create the mythology of the warrior from history and offer a heroic context to the struggle for meaning and happiness upon the return from battle. It is an attempt to develop a narrative of hope and redemption for those who feel like they let themselves and others down, even though they did their best or, indeed, did nothing wrong. A soldier returns home from battle but has brought the war back with him. He stares off into the distance in what is called the "1,000-yard stare." People in these groups are surprised that this stare has a long-standing place in human history; indeed, it is mentioned in the Greek play by Sophocles called *Ajax*, which is more than 2,000 years old. (Ajax is unable to find contentment in his family or friends and remains hyper-alert to false threats. He cannot heal his invisible wounds and kills himself.)

The gay community can learn a few things from the treatment of soldiers by military psychiatrists. The military teaches veterans that a man who is worn down is not at all "weak."' He is having a normal reaction to discrimination and stigmatization, especially if he is HIV positive. He has a heart. Only a sociopathic man can remain impervious to a lifetime of tragedy from the AIDS crisis, discrimination in the workplace, bullying, and ongoing stigmatization. Gay men need a home in which to rest. They need alternatives to drugs and alcohol. Rehabs for gay men work. Gay and lesbian meetings of Twelve Step programs also help. The community must act to create a home and not just a series of streets lined with gay bars. Veterans often are only allowed to offer a sanitized version of what happened to them. People do not want to know any of the unpleasantness of real battle. Similarly, we are led to believe that gay life can be a sanitized affair of happy people who love to create, have terrific imaginations, and are at the center of the creative flow in theater, entertainment, fashion, and design. This is not true and it is a naïve and sanitized version. We need to focus on the parts of gay life that lack continuity, the parts of gay life that cause isolation, and the tragic pasts of many gay men that have been concealed for way too long.

Furthermore, leaders in the gay community needs to tell younger gay men that they do not need to get wrapped up in CMA and HIV by the time they are thirty. To take a neutral stand on this self-destructive behavior is to wallow in the trauma. Gay men can and should make healthy choices, and these healthy choices should be supported wholeheartedly by the community. Gay life does not have to be lived with HIV medications, occasional bouts with CMA, and repeated stints in rehabs. The community should offer an ideal.

PTSD caused by death in battle or death of a loved one from HIV or AIDS is th same. Trauma comes from a sense that develops when the optimism and promise of youth encounters a cold and hardened reality. The reality is that society, as far as we have come, is not yet ready to offer gay and bisexual men a seat at the table, especially in Asia. This truth can cause people to feel

A HISTORY OF PTSD: HELP FOR THE WEARY HEART AND A WAY TO A NEW HOME

The American Psychiatric Association defines post-traumatic stress disorder (PTSD) as an anxiety (emotional) disorder that stems from a particular incident evoking significant stress such as a car accident, sexual assault, or other traumatic experiences including combat, physical beatings, or nearness to someone who has died. This disorder has been with us for thousands of years. It seems people do not yet know how to react to sudden, violent, or emotionally cruel trauma. Greek historians speak of soldiers becoming blinded by the sight of death even though they had no physical injury. Others speak of soldiers who lose the will to fight on and become ashamed of themselves for being "cowards." This fear certainly goes beyond the experience of war. For example, people often cannot sleep for days after being in a house fire. Others cannot bring themselves to go into a car after a terrible automobile accident. Some gay men come to see all men as a threat after being beaten up by a group of men in a gay-bashing incident. The result of all of these events is disturbed sleep, depression, rage-filled behavior, heart palpitations, anxiety, and an incessant search for home. It is a loss of will to fight on. It is a loss of purpose which causes soldiers to consider self-inflicted injury.

The German term for PTSD translates into "homesickness." In French, it is "sickness for the country." In Spanish, it is "being broken." They called those traumatized Civil War veterans in another world "weary hearts," people who would just wander around and remain homeless.

Is the desire by many wounded gay men to contract HIV through unsafe sex another form of having a "weary heart"? Is it a form of self-inflicted injury? The raft of statistics in the gay community shows rising HIV rates all over as well as rising or persistent drug and alcohol abuse (especially among gay males). We need to go down this road, as so many can relate to the suggestion in *The Velvet Rage* that many gay men suffer PTSD. This is especially true of older gay men who have witnessed numerous friends and lovers die from AIDS. Let's also remember that, although the illness can now be treated, HIV continues to be a chronic condition with serious medical side effects. And let's remember that the official medical term for HIV is a "pandemic." And 60 percent of new cases are in the gay community.

So, what should the community do with this startling realization that PTSD is all too common among its members? For soldiers who have seen people killed in battle or in accidents and for gay people who have been victims of physical, sexual, or verbal abuse, there is too much discounting in society. This in itself is destructive and reinforces the problem. These already troubled people can lose self-confidence and self-respect when others respond to their pain by telling them to simply shape up and pull themselves up by their bootstraps.

Where is *home* for the gay man? Where is that safe place he can heal? Emotional stress can occur during a moment of sexual abuse at twelve or thirteen. It can occur during a beating at sixteen by a father or by others who taunt an effeminate boy. It can occur when a person sees someone else die of AIDS or learns that he has tested positive for HIV. When there is no emotional outlet, drugs and alcohol seem to be a good solution. They numb the feelings of homelessness and isolation.

How can the rainbow warrior be convinced that other solutions can indeed heal the weary heart when he knows no better? How can the gay man escape a sense of sadness, weariness, pessimism, irritability, and lack of attention that is part and parcel of a community where drug and alcohol addiction rates are three to four times higher than in the heterosexual population? Addiction is not weakness of character. It is an accumulation of rejection, stigmatization, and lack of acceptance of "who and what" a gay man is. Life is tough for everyone, but being a gay man in a society that questions his masculinity, that includes overt or covert bullying, and that allows abuse and discrimination to persist can wear a person down and lead to cynicism and pessimism, especially when it was society that caused the gay person to live a double life.

weary, rootless, and broken. Or it can be a reason to bring about more change and create a home where one can. Gay men need to find a way home in a world that may never fully accept them. Otherwise, they will feel superfluous, cynical, and bewildered. They cannot count on their own families to fully support them, so they need to create family in other ways.

If gay men become detached from all of the sickness and addiction in the gay community, they should not be overly critical toward their own people. This is a perfectly normal response to the exceptionally high levels of substance abuse in the community. Sometimes, we detach in order to survive. It is a kind of numbing and it has a price. The solution may be to jump in to volunteer work to help the gay community heal. Nothing brings about more healing than working to heal that which bothers us most. Gay men who dislike their own community may come to love it through their own efforts of helping it to change. Pretending not to give a damn about the problems in the gay community is itself soul-destroying. For courageous veterans helping those with PTSD or gay people in the gay community, it is fundamentally human trait that volunteerism seems to allow a person to "forget himself" for a while. He can detach from his past pain by helping another person who suffers from the same painful trauma. Veterans working with other veterans helps them to detach from painful memories and move on with life. Alcoholics working with other alcoholics help them to detach form the pain and anguish of addiction and move on with life. Can it be that we need a whole new paradigm of volunteerism in the gay community to allow gay and bisexual men to help one another and detach from past pain of bullying, stigmatization, discrimination, and death of loved ones from HIV and AIDS? Can the gay community overcome a failure of imagination during a heightening epidemic of HIV and drug and alcohol addiction and create programs in the gay community like www.soldieron.org.au to help those walking wounded who suffer from HIV, drug addiction, anxiety and loneliness? Can the medical community drum up the courage to stop using hyper-politically correct language and publish papers which suggest programs which encourage gay men to get into volunteer action and which can be done on a large scale within the gay community? It can't hurt and the programs in place so far have done very little to stem the tide either of drug addiction or HIV proliferation. The question is: can grass roots activity by veterans to help the tens of thousands with veterans with PTSD be transferred into the gay community to help the tens of thousands of gay men with PTSD?

Shame is toxic. When gay men experience shame about who they are and shame about their community, they essentially forget who they are and their purpose. It robs them of joy. It lowers their standard of thinking and feeling. In conditions that include a great deal of substance abuse and unsafe sex leading to HIV transmission, facing reality and helping to change attitudes in a constructive way keeps the spirit alive. Even being a gay man who stays clean and sober may have profound consequences, giving others something to aspire to.

If a gay man is put through the ringer of substance abuse, unsafe sex, and tantalizing promiscuity, he should let himself off the hook since these behaviors are often a sane response to a world that is often unfair and cruel to the gay man, especially in places like Asia, Africa, and Latin America. Redemption comes at us from all directions and at all time, especially from the depths. The heroes are the ones who rise up from the ashes. Rainbow warriors are the ones who come back from the abyss just as much as they lead from the front. We cannot know who will come back from the abyss just as it is impossible to predict who will lead the gay community from the front. Often, they are the same people. We all have a breaking point but all of us are also equally capable of reaching down and finding great courage from a higher power.

A common response to the exceptionally high substance abuse rates in the gay community is to join the party. Another common response is to try to get better and make healthy choices and make a difference. The community needs to focus on what it means to be an individual (focus, accomplishment, expression of emotion, pride) rather than letting the group decay into self-destruction, denial, shame, and death. Having closed himself in order to survive, the gay man (and the gay community) needs to work his way back to the human job of emotion, reaching out, accomplishment, or help. This requires some re-creation of family. The ultimate cure for PTSD in the gay community is, however, to work toward an end to discrimination, stigmatization, and hatred of those who are gay, bisexual, or lesbian.[3]

The word "trauma" is Greek for wound. Michael Meade, an author, storyteller, and scholar on mythology who has created programs for veterans, makes the profound insight that every wound is like a mouth—it must speak its truth. Meade argues that trauma must be given a voice and the truth must be told. He is working to help soldiers with PTSD—more than 1,000 are diagnosed with PTSD each week—cope with psychological stress caused by a long war.

Meade uses the following methods to help veterans. During his program's four-day retreats, he uses mythology from Ireland, Greece, and India as a context to give veterans a comfort zone to unload their traumatic experiences and make sense of what happened. They sing chants, write about their experiences, and recite poetry about surviving battle and the heroism of war. He asks them to reflect on how other cultures treat their returning soldiers and makes the case that many other cultures treat their veterans much better. He creates a safe place for veterans to exit the "Underworld" and to give themselves permission to leave behind their dead comrades and the parts of themselves that were lost to battle.

Other groups (including theater groups sponsored by the Pentagon) have taken their cue from Meade and perform plays like *Ajax* (the troupe is called the Theater of War) for thousands of people across the country.

In a later section, we'll explore the remarkable similarities between the healing of the trauma of war and the healing of the trauma of sexual/physical abuse and the madness of reckless addictive behavior. Recovery is an attempt to breach the limbo of "war" and return to a normal life. We will see how the type of activities described above can be adopted to help gay men exit the Underworld and stop dragging back bodies or memories from the dead past and leaving them in the living room.

Meade's work helps remove the stigma of PTSD by showing that it has been occurring for thousands of years. Also, by bringing this difficult issue into a theater setting, it lets the person view himself from a distance through the characters on the stage. The drama of the theater creates a safe distance.

DEALING WITH BRAIN CHEMISTRY

The ability of the military to treat anxiety, depression, memory loss, and the symptoms of post-traumatic stress disorder has become one of the most important battles of the post-war period.[4] Currently, the Pentagon is trying to develop a brain chip to treat PTSD in soldiers and veterans that could bring sweeping changes to the way depression and anxiety is treated for millions of Americans, not just veterans. It is attempting to reach into the brain's soft tissue in order to record, predict, and potentially treat anxiety and depression. This is similar to successful treatments for Parkinson's disease. The military is involving the University of California, San Francisco, and the Lawrence Livermore Laboratory in this research. On top of profound developments in medications, there are myriad other ways to help all types of wounded warriors rebuild a normal life.[5]

PTSD AND THE GAY OR BISEXUAL MAN

The interesting part of this discussion on military PTSD is that, while we are grateful to veterans for their service and for the sacrifice they made in hellish conditions, PTSD affects a wide swath of the community and is brought on by a wide array of traumatic experiences. Indeed, one veteran connected to the story in the article mentioned above made the point that "PTSD affects police, fire and EMS, surgeons, nurses, all fields that experience major trauma either to them or out."[6] Victims of long-term domestic violence can develop it. Living in a bad neighborhood where there is homicide and criminality can create it.

Other episodes and situations can create PTSD: overdosing or being near someone who overdoses in front of you; being in prison; being in a horrible car accident while drunk or high. Or, in the case of the topic in chapter 3, being sexually abused as a child (and/or being physically or verbally abused) and dealing with rehabilitation from drug abuse. And, if a gay man is over forty years old, he likely knows someone—probably a close friend or lover—who has died from complications of AIDS. Violent episodes during addiction, HIV/AIDS, physical and sexual abuse, bullying, as well as workplace discrimination or harassment are common themes that bleed through the fabric of the lives of many gay men in modern times. If this is not a recipe for even a mild form of PTSD for gay, bisexuals, and lesbians, nothing is.

In his book *The Velvet Rage*, Alan Downs makes the case that gay men are four times more likely to develop problems with substance abuse. In addition, he reports that "a sizable minority of gay men were sexually abused as children and larger numbers report a rape-like experience."[7] As a therapist who frequently treated gay men in therapy, he also comes to the same conclusion as many studies do. The simple reality staring us in the face is that gay men who have experienced physical or sexual abuse as a child, irresponsible drug

THE EFFECT OF JACK'S SEXUAL ABUSE IN ADULTHOOD—AND THE HEALING PROCESS

Jack learned that many men who were abused as boys can act according to a "script." If their first sexual encounters are considered taboo, "risky," "unacceptable," subject to severe punishment or reprisal, or imply shamefulness, then adult sexual encounters with other consenting adults can take on this same tone. Adult survivors of sexual abuse often "re-create" the emotions surrounding sex as an adult with those emotions he felt during his first sexual encounters. He seems locked in that trauma.

When sex is seen as a taboo and subject to punishment (especially from an adolescent's point of view), then sexual liaisons as an adult can frequently evolve into dark activities that involve psychological elements of taboo, punishment, illicitness, and self-destruction. As we've seen in this book, gay men who have been sexually abused have higher incidence of HIV infection, and now we know why.

In therapy, Jack learned that he needed to confront the scary and threatening. The script he learned during adolescence is that sex results in the perpetrator being removed from the scene. Without any counseling or candid discussion with the family, it resulted in a dirty secret that lingered and was somehow shoved under the carpet for many years. Furthermore, where there is one episode of sexual abuse, there are often many more in the family unit that go unspoken.

After receiving treatment and therapy, Jack went back to a relative he thought might also have been abused by his brother, and he helped this person find healing as well. First, he listened to the "mouth" that needed to tell about the "wound." Then he shared some advice that was given to him in therapy. Helping others to heal and trying to forgive the perpetrator seem to be two key ways to escape the dysfunctional sexual adult narrative.

taking, or the death of a close one from complications of HIV/AIDS bring many symptoms of PTSD into their relationships. Here are the tell-tale signs of PTSD which generally revolve around emotional numbness and hypervigilance. We have a strange inclination to relive the trauma. Do we have this perverse but necessary need to understand it fully before we can let go of it? Do we relive trauma perhaps as a way to get through to the other side? Do we familiarize ourselves with it in order to overcome it? It seems so. Another mechanism we use is to make efforts to avoid thinking about the trauma. Alcohol and drugs are a viable alternative for this. Indeed, this reinforces the old adage which says, "By the time I had my first drink, I needed it."

We make efforts to avoid situations that arouse memories. Victims of family trauma (verbal, physical, or sexual abuse) will cut themselves off from all family members for a period of time until the trauma recedes. Another way to avoid the emotions is to have blackouts with regard to periods in childhood when trauma occurred. The subconscious has a remarkable and uncanny way of offering us memories when we are ready to deal with them. Blackouts are the mind's way of protecting us from memories which are too hot to handle.

Trauma makes us have reduced interest in important activities. Many gay men who have experienced the death of a lover or a friend from AIDS—or who has been marginalized by discrimination, stigmatization, or bullying—can become hardened and cynical, experiencing reduced interest in career, relationships, family, and hobbies. In addition to blackouts, we have limited emotions about life in general. This limited emotional range can stem from earlier memories of death from AIDS in the 1980s and 1990s, angry fathers who dislike a son being gay, and overt discrimination at work. Shutting down memories means shutting down emotional bandwidth.

A common result of reliving past trauma and shutting down emotionally is a feeling that there are no future prospects. Gay white men certainly can feel this, but this may be even more acutely felt by gay black men. A sense of doom comes from being marginalized and from depression mixed with abuse. It is a small wonder that one of the hallmarks of this disturbing combination of emotional responses is hypervigilance. This is a sense of mistrust and a general unwillingness to engage anyone on an emotional level requiring trust. If I experience physical or emotional abuse in adolescence, I am likely to have these painful memories in what many call the hard drive. It remains there and must be given a voice in order to heal. Many wise men conclude that forgiveness of the perpetrator is essential to overcome this sense of doom and hyper-vigilance.[8]

HEALING WITH THE GROUP— HELPING ONE'S SELF BY HELPING OTHERS TO HEAL

As with anyone who has post-traumatic distress disorder, victims of sexual abuse replay the episode in their heads over and over again. Some incest survivors say they think of the episode every day for years. Breaking this cycle often requires being in a safe environment with a professional and metaphorically traveling back to the home in a psychological journey.

Before we discuss how to do this, let's return to the four questions that the wounded warrior returning from battle asks himself. In a process aimed at understanding the past and mourning the loss of innocence, normality, and a healthy sexual self-image, the gay man in recovery who has also been sexually or physically abused can ask himself these same questions to get at the heart of the stress disorder and help him progress on the difficult road to recovery:

1. Guilt: Why did I survive the event? What happened to the other guy? Why him and not me?

   This question arises all too frequently. Some gay men—as well as straight men at a young age—enjoyed the sexual encounter and went back for more. Yet, the abuser suddenly disappeared. He was chased away or arrested. The victim experiences a feeling of survivor's guilt because someone else was punished or disappeared while he went along with the activity and had formed some kind of attachment to the abuser.
2. Remorse: Couldn't I have done more to prevent the event? Am I incompetent after all the experience I have?

   This is also a common result of abuse, especially for boys who grew up to be bisexual or heterosexual. They asked themselves over and over again how they could have changed the incident to push away the predator. They express remorse about being a "weakling." Straight men have told me again and again that they felt like they were a "pussy" for not stopping the incident. To resolve these feelings, self-forgiveness must be a part of the forgiveness process if the person is to eventually accept the event and move on in his life. This part of the process becomes much easier if the stigma of sexual abuse is removed and society recognizes the true prevalence of sexual abuse. Indeed, this issue could be resolved much easier if sexual abuse was brought out of the closet and discussed in a calm and rational manner.
3. Shame: I ducked and the other guy didn't and now he's dead. What about my other friends who have fallen around me? Is it all just dumb luck?

   Many gay men in adulthood know of another friend who was sexually abused (possibly by the same abuser) and this other person just never seemed to "get better." That person may have gone down the road of reckless sexual encounters or prostitution and may have contracted HIV—or even died in mysterious circumstances. Older gay men who are in recovery and are HIV-negative believe they have dodged a bullet and somehow escaped the fate of a slew of friends who are dead.
4. Cowardice: Why didn't I do more to prevent the damage in all of my adult relationships? Am I a coward?

   In addition to the actual act of sexual abuse and the seeming inability to do anything to stop it, many men who are abusing substances or acting irresponsibly in sexual activity ask themselves why they continue to lack the courage to put a halt to their self-destructive lifestyles. They see themselves as powerless over various aspects of their lives—from forming or maintaining relationships, holding down a steady job, or staying in one place for any length of time.

So, we can see that the experience of PTSD is different for these two populations—the "wounded warrior" back from the Middle East grieving the loss of comrades and the middle-aged gay man grieving his own losses, including his childhood innocence, bullying and discrimination, and many friends who died from complications of HIV—but has striking similarities.

CREATING A SAFE ENVIRONMENT TO RESCUE AND NURTURE THE ABUSED CHILD WITHIN

Many years ago, I worked with a group of men who were all victims of childhood sexual abuse and who were also in recovery from drug addiction. I had created the group alongside a well-trained and experienced therapist. The group of eight men met for several months to deal with their toxic shame and low self-esteem stemming from not only the sexual abuse but also the shame of their own sexual acting out as adults. We created a safe and friendly environment where the men were encouraged to share their experience and to help others in the group in a constructive way.

The stigma of sexual abuse was quickly eliminated because everyone in the group had been sexually abused and because the group leader clearly communicated just how common abuse is in society. Each person was allowed to share his experience with the group in this safe and unhurried environment. I am convinced that hearing another person's experience of abuse is a way for the listener to gain distance from his own experience and start to heal.

After some weeks, each person was given a chance to confront his abuser in an imaginary way by sitting across from an empty chair and reading a written letter to the abuser seated there. In general, this worked extremely well to provide closure, and all of the letters were powerful and generally civil. Through this process, the group healed together, not alone. Several of the individuals in the group were also in Twelve Step programs and reminded others who were not that a major tenet of working Step Nine—the Step focusing on forgiveness—is that the forgiveness is not for the abuser but rather for the individual who is doing the forgiving. The process of forgiveness is where we do *not* excuse the behavior but we forgive, or let go of, the behavior. It is a way out of the Underworld of shame and toxicity where the victim carries the abuser around like a tattered security blanket. The security blanket of shame is dropped and a new life of authenticity can begin.

The third part of this involved another exercise where each person (and this can be done as a group) took an imagined journey back to the place in his home where, as children, he felt most safe and at ease. This could be somewhere in the yard, in his bedroom, in front of the TV, or even a secret hiding place. Then, the group coordinator asks each person to bring that child out of that safe place from his childhood home and to nurture that frightened child as an adult in a safe environment. That meant creating a safe environment as an adult where the "child within" can learn to trust, play, relax, and have a happy life. If the adult continues to maintain a reckless lifestyle where there is no real safety, the child within cannot have relief and will continue to mourn subconsciously at the dark and misty edges of the man's consciousness. This childhood trauma demands a voice and some relief. It demands a mourning process. And creating a safe place for the "child within" seems to be a good place to start.[9]

Furthermore, the therapist with whom I coordinated the group made a wise observation. He asked each man who was having difficulty in talking to touch his knees to remind himself that he was now an adult and not that same child who was abused. He also invited the men to take off their shoes and socks, and dig their feet into the carpet to remind themselves they were adult men with adult feet—that is, they were no longer small children with small feet. They were now capable, if they wanted, of taking care of themselves and creating a safe environment as adults. They no longer had to feel like a frightened and wounded boy in a man's body.

THERAPY AND TWELVE STEP GROUPS HAVE THE SAME AIMS: FORGIVENESS OF SELF AND OTHERS

Some people have told me they used the Twelve Step program to gain the courage to forgive abusers of all sorts. Also, the Twelve Step philosophy asks each adult in recovery what their role was in the conflict. An adult knows that he or she has no part in the sexual abuse as a boy or girl. His or her part in the abuse is limited to what he or she did with the abuse *in adulthood*. Adults can use sex to repeat the feelings of a taboo and forbidden experience in hundreds of unhealthy sexual encounters with anonymous partners. They can see sex as a risky activity and engage in risky behaviors during sex. After all, there is a sense within an adolescent young adult who is, say fifteen or sixteen years old, that there is danger in engaging in sex with an adult. They might carry this emotion of riskiness into adulthood as they form ideas of sexual activity as an adult with other adults. Risky activity in adulthood could include public sex, random pickups, prostitution, and unsafe sex. This unsafe sex offers a heightened sense of riskiness and may be a throwback to the times when they were having inappropriate sexual activity with adults or engaging in unwanted sexual encounters with adults. This desire to equate sex with riskiness may explain the connection between those with HIV and unwanted sexual encounters.

Breaking the link between sex and riskiness is the key. Turning the act of sex into a meaningful expression of intimacy is a tall order. But the starting point must be looking into the adolescent sexual conduct and finding a way for the adult man or woman to gain forgiveness for the self and for the perpetrator. The quote at the beginning of this chapter from Marion Davies has a profound message about human nature. As long as we are down in the gutter cursing the oppressor, we can never rise up to gain a sense of independence. We are slaves to rage and anger and self-pity. These emotions are the bread and butter of addiction.

These raging emotions stir together to form a cauldron of anxiety, alienation, and self-loathing which often result in risky sexual activity that is a repeat of the trauma. Alcohol or drugs are used to quell the memories of the behavior of the 'night before.' Drug use with relaxants helps to prevent any contact with adolescent memories which may be associated with humiliation ("I couldn't get away"), self-blame ("I liked it and I am ashamed") or self-condemnation ("I had sex with my older brother and he was banished from the family unit"). Often, these people engage in risky sexual behavior that is a response to past trauma, i.e., repeating the traumatic behavior in different forms because it somehow feels good. Often, alcohol or drug use can quell the rage and anger at the adults who should have been in a position to do something and didn't (or, perversely, may have somehow encouraged it).

In the Twelve Step process, one is able to find self-forgiveness for the psychological and physical damage he caused to himself. He is told by his AA sponsor that the forgiveness was *not* for the abuser but for *him* to heal and regain a sense of his individual self as a healthy sexual adult capable of creating a safe environment. The adage is we forgive but do not forget. The forgiveness is for the person who was abused in order to let this person off the hook for spending his adult life as a victim. Forgiveness of the abuser or oppressor short circuits the cycle of self-sabotage and allows a person to get on with his life. Victims 'drink at' their oppressors. They take a poison and hope that the oppressor dies. This is ultimately fatal and can be stopped through a process of forgiveness for the abuser and the self.

SEEKING A GAY AND BISEXUAL MYTHOLOGY AND A NEW DIALOGUE

Too many gay men get to their thirties and forties exhausted and beaten down. They are all wrung out! Many enter rehab and try to get sober but they do not find any heroes or gay mythology for which they can feel pride. It is not enough to just cope and have a career. Life demands more than this. Gay life demands a mythology akin to the way in which soldiers can make sense of the carnage of battle. Gay men need to make sense of their own past of abuse, discrimination, bullying, absence of male mentors, and too great an emphasis on drugs and alcohol as an organizing principle in the gay community.

If we stop to think about the number of gay men who have made stunning achievements in society and find a way to create a patchwork quilt of the profound achievement to human life by gays, bisexuals, and lesbians, it would be staggering. The patchwork that we as gay men know all too well is the AIDS quilt, an ever growing and beautiful monument to the hundreds of thousands of fallen gay men who have died from HIV-related illnesses. This is a great achievement and is a way for the community to grieve as a group. It needs to be continued and expanded. We must honor the dead and grieve the loss.

At the same time, though, we must honor the living and create a source of pride and purpose by designating heroes and icons. The gay community needs to create a patchwork of portraits of gay men and women's staggering contribution to the arts, literature, Broadway, technology, poetry, economics, science, sports, and many more human endeavors. These are men who have won the Pulitzer Prize, the Booker Prize, the Nobel Prize, the Academy Award, the Tony Award, and many other internationally recognized awards

RAINBOW WARRIORS

It is hard to know when the collective psyche (whether it is soldiers who mourn the deaths of young comrades in arms or gay men who mourn the deaths of hundreds of thousands of young men from HIV-related illnesses) is on a path toward healing and is ready to celebrate the living rather than the dead. In the case of PTSD for soldiers returning from the Middle East, it is early days. For the gay community, there is still a lot of behavior that has an odor of PTSD and yet, there is a generation emerging from the tragic mess of AIDS who seems ready to grab onto something else. That 'something else' is an authenticity and a set of values which is a move away from alcohol, drugs, and promiscuity and toward a more sane and rational design for living.

The question before us is this: Is this a time of change and is the way forward to create a cultural patchwork quilt of inspiration for the living? This may seem controversial, but this is what I sense. Something is in the air that calls out for mentors, leaders, new values, and a fresh compass for the gay community. A generation of walking wounded may not know how to do this, but humans seem to re-create values all the time. Gay men may be doing this right now.

of excellence. The greats that come to mind in our age include composer Stephen Sondheim, composer Leonard Bernstein, artist Elton John, politician Barney Frank, athlete Billy Jean King, and director John Waters. Famous dead gay men include artists Michelangelo, Da Vinci, and Andy Warhol, poet Walt Whitman, scientist Francis Bacon, writer Herman Melville, economist John Maynard Keynes, UN Secretary General Dag Hammskjold, TE Lawrence (Lawrence of Arabia), composer Cole Porter, Harvey Milk, and many others. The list goes on and on and yet the gay community is rightfully and justifiably in a grieving stage for all the fallen heroes from HIV/AIDS. The question in front of us is: is it time to stop remembering people for how they died and start remembering them for how they lived?

LEARNING HOW TO CHANGE ADULT BEHAVIOR BY FOLLOWING CHILDHOOD ADVICE

It may sound strange, but the advice we give to children to avoid unwelcome sexual advances may be the same straightforward suggestions that adults need in order to make behavior modifications. If we take the literal advice for children and make it figurative advice for adults, we'll have a good starting point for breaking the sexual narrative of abuse that adults all too often get trapped in. (Recall earlier that I made the point that humans have an eerie tendency to repeat trauma that remains unspoken or unresolved.) Children are often given four instructions to avoid sexual predators:

1. Identify dangerous situations and places.
2. Refuse an abuser's approach.
3. Break off the interaction.
4. Summon help from an adult.

These four rudimentary instructions for children can be an intriguing gateway for dealing with adults who are suffering from the trauma of childhood sexual abuse. Young people are often given the following advice in order to break off any association that could lead to trouble:

1. **Identify dangerous situations and places.** To avoid abuse, young people are told to talk with their family members and other responsible adults about situations that could lead to trouble. Being alone in unfamiliar places is a bad idea. Congregating in neighborhoods, homes, or social settings where there is alcohol or drugs is also unwise. Avoiding adults who make overly sexual suggestions or who are verbally abusive is a good idea.

As I was reading this, I was struck because this is exactly what can be standard advice for an adult survivor of abuse. Adults need to be aware of the kinds of adults with whom they surround themselves. They should be aware that being in an alcohol- and drug-filled club at one o'clock in the morning is generally a very bad idea. They should be aware of the kinds of self-destructive, gossipy, or demanding relatives or siblings who should be avoided in adulthood.[10] There is a need to stop being a doormat when it comes to tolerating mean-spirited or negative behavior which can suck the life out of a person. It means refusing to be around other people who tear down others with sarcasm. (The literal meaning of sarcasm is to "tear the flesh").

2. **Refuse an abuser's approach**. Again, this is advice to a child but it is profoundly simple but appropriate advice for an adult as well. Adult survivors of abuse need to be aware of and avoid abusive people. Some adults will never stop being an "abuser" or opting for manipulative cruelty. They need to be avoided.

   Adults need to have an "eyes wide open" attitude about abusive adults, because there is often some perverse comfort in falling into the arms of an abuser. If nothing else, there is a familiar ring of childhood experience. For that is what we knew growing up in abusive homes.[11]

3. **Break off the interaction.** Children are told to break off the interaction if they sense danger. How true this is for adults as well! Too often, adult survivors of abuse stay in relationships involving abuse because they think that they will never find another person who will love them. Their self-esteem is so low that they think no one else could possibly love them the way this guy "loves" them. Although easy to say but difficult to do, breaking off interaction with an abuser is a vital action for recovery.[12] It requires the courage to know: a) that the person has enough self-worth to break off the relationship in the first place, and b) that the person has enough self-confidence to know that there is someone else out there that will (and should) treat them with dignity.
4. **Summon help from an adult.** A child can run to the parent or guardian to ask for help to fend off a potential abuser. But adult survivors of abuse are often at sea about what kind of resources are available when they want to summon help. Therapy with a qualified counselor is advised. However, as we mentioned earlier, there are a tiny handful of trained counselors and millions of gay men who are adrift in a sea of substance abuse, trauma from childhood abuse or bullying, and undiagnosed PTSD. Recognition by society about the level of sexual abuse is an important first step.

A dialogue in the gay community needs to start about mental health issues that plague the community through no fault of its own. Many gay men grow into adulthood <u>without</u> adequate coping mechanisms, strong, masculine and sensible male mentors, a healthy sense of their own masculinity; a healthy view of sex, and without support from the community, church, or the workplace.

No wonder why the incidence of substance abuse is so common! Times are changing, of course, but society needs to ask why the incidence of substance abuse is not changing as much as it should. Alas, HIV transmission and CMA use seem to be on the rise. It is time for a grassroots program akin to programs for wounded warriors returning from battle. These programs should include the following:

- Expanded suicide prevention hotlines
- Greater information and prevention programs for CMA abuse
- More cooperation with law enforcement for CMA interdiction
- More public space for gay and bisexual men to have Twelve Step meetings or other support groups
- Active creation of groups for gay men recovering from sexual abuse
- More programs like "contingency management" for indigent gay men who receive groceries in exchange for maintaining sobriety (this is cheaper than long-term treatment)
- Public campaigns about PTSD in areas frequented by gay men
- A greater level of communication between counselors and doctors to encourage a dialogue about which medications are appropriate for men in recovery and which are addictive. Active discussion about differences between SSRIs and benzodiazepines is a good start. Some Twelve Step–related groups are ignorant of the difference, for instance
- Information campaigns for acceptance of gay men and women in the workplace
- Integrated discussion and seminars for doctors, psychiatrists, and counselors to communicate more with each other about treatment programs for victims of sexual abuse

Other programs are being developed for soldiers returning from battle—and should be considered for treatment for gay and bisexual addicted men. These men may be dealing with traumatic pasts, a split self, exposure to friends or lovers who have died and/or who may also have been victimized by homophobia, arrest, bullying or beatings. Examples of this include:[13]

1. The most successful is CBT which aims to bring up the trauma in talk therapy through "exposure." This is generally successful, although the painful memories cause many to quit before the therapy can be effective.

2. Eye movement desensitization and reprocessing (EMDR) is still an experimental treatment and involves moving eyes from side to side while discussing traumatic memories. It is a more physical version of talk therapy and allows a person to process distressing memories.
3. Mindfulness methods are being implemented to train a person to stay in the moment. A book like Eckhart Tolle's *The Power of Now* is just one example. The Twelve Step movement has a powerful foundational premise which is to stay sober and in the moment. The phrase "One day at a time" is not just a cliché but a foundation of the program.
4. It is interesting that researchers on PTSD among soldiers concluded that yoga was no better a therapy than talk therapy. Combining physical activity with talk therapy seems an ideal situation.
5. Meditation programs which are repeated mantras "loving kindness" have also been tried in military circles.
6. Other activities which can help include group scuba, horseback, dancing, music therapy, tai chi, and companion dogs.
7. Treatments like acupuncture and Native American healing can also help.

CMA AS A DRUG OF CHOICE FOR GAY MEN

Like some combat soldiers who get addicted to the high of danger and death, adult survivors of sexual abuse also have a narrative that sex in adulthood should be dangerous, forbidden, illicit, or carry the potential for serious consequences. In this way, it is no accident that crystal methamphetamine (CMA) is a common drug for gay men. An inordinate number of these men have experienced sexual abuse (or carried on sexual activity with a brother or cousin similar in age, which they find to be shameful). As a result, they may be caught in a cycle of shame and drag their sexual past into the present and repeat the shameful sexual activity.

A drug like CMA lets the inhibitions melt away and allows these traumatic events to meld into dark sexual fantasies in a way that alcohol, cocaine, or marijuana generally do not. While on CMA, some adults may want to play out "incest fantasies" with adult sex partners as a way to live in the past trauma. Various forms of illicit sex—public sexual activity, unsafe sex with strangers, bondage sex involving pain, sadomasochistic fantasy, rape fantasy, kidnapping fantasy—all can play a role in repeating the past trauma. In its darkest form, the most dangerous narrative involves seeking out children as sex partners and repeating the past in a literal way. Tragically, such patterns often do repeat themselves. The consequences of this are, of course, likely incarceration and a lifelong brand of sex offender.

THE PATH TO FORGIVENESS—PITY FOR THE PERPETRATOR

Some consider it sinister to grant forgiveness to a man or a woman who sexually abuses a child. Yet, it is my experience in working with hundreds of adult survivors of sexual abuse that it is possible, quite common, and ultimately life-giving. Again, the forgiveness of the person is *not* for the benefit of the abuser but so that the wounded adult can find healing, clarity of purpose, and healthy adult relationships. The forgiveness is for them—not for the abuser. Forgiveness cuts the bonds. Forgiveness is the way to pick up the key that will release victims from their self-constructed prison and allow them to finally move on with their lives. The person forgives but does not forget.

At its heart, forgiveness involves pardoning the self as well as the other person. They are two sides of the same coin. In my own vulnerability, forgiveness is found. I know fathers whose sons were murdered and they found forgiveness for the murderer. I know a man who was sexually abused by his father and he eventually found forgiveness for his father. They were able to do this by forgiving themselves for their own weakness and by finding pity for the abuser. We are all in this together. Healing comes from forgiveness and helping others to heal. This is a time-honored truism—it has been around for as long as mankind has been writing about healing, progress, and forgiveness. Forgiveness of the self and of others lies in realizing that all of us—convicts and men of letters—are made of the same clay. We are all wounded, vulnerable, and broken in some ways. And we all heal in the same ways.

NOTES

1. Joseph E. O. Newtona, W. Brian McPhersona, Peggy T. Ackermana, Jerry G. Jonesa, and Roscoe A Dykmana, "Prevalence of Post-Traumatic Stress Disorder and Other Psychiatric Diagnoses in Three Groups of Abused Children (Sexual, Physical, and Both)," *Child Abuse and Neglec*t 22, no. 8 (August 1998): 759–74.

2. Joseph H. Beitchman, et. al, "A Review of the Long-Term Effects of Child Sexual Abuse," *Child Abuse and Neglect* 16, no. 1 (1992): 101–18.

3. Some of the ideas in this reflection came from an article in a newsletter called *The Veteran.* It is by Jack Bentley and is entitled "A Short History of PTSD: From Thermophlae to Hue: Soldiers Have Always Had a Disturbing Reaction to War," (1991).

4. Patrick Tucker, "The Military Is Building Brain Chips to Treat PTSD," *Defense One Newsletter,* May 25, 2014.

5. Another excellent treatment of this is in Jaron Lanier's riveting book *Who Owns the Future?* (2014, Simon & Schuster) in which he opines about the future of the

intersection of big data, chemistry, and biology. He suggests we could all have a chip in our bodies that not only monitors all blood activity but also dispenses treatments, vitamins, mood stabilizers, and other required medications.

6. This comment was among the comments in the blog following the article above.

7. Downes, *Velvet Rage,* 142.

8. Ibid., 134.

9. See also *A Gift to Myself* by Charles Whitfield. This is the workbook compendium for his original book *Healing the Child Within* (Health Communications, 1989, 2006).

10. A helpful book for this is called *Living Sober* published by Alcoholics Anonymous World Services. It is a handy guide to learn how to avoid "slippery places."

11. There is often an unconscious desire to fall into the arms of an abuser precisely in the midst of painful but ultimately rewarding work on past abuse. Some people think this is a confirmation of just how "twisted" they are, but it is a natural response to the unnatural circumstance of adolescent abuse. If adults hang in there and give the process time—even a few months—it undoubtedly gets better. If a person finds themselves eating more, watching TV more, or smoking more, this is better than getting into a tangled relationship with an abusive person.

12. Al-Anon is a great program in this regard. It teaches the person in an abusive relationship with an addict to detach with love and protect the physical and emotional space of a person who is trying to heal and create an individual. Individuation is at the core of the Al-Anon program and is achieved through a spiritual experience with a Higher Power of choice.

13. Excerpts from In Depth: "US Veterans Try New Ways To Heal the Wounds of War," by Michael Phillips and Shirley Wang, *Wall Street Journal*, September 15, 2014.

Chapter Six

The Psychological. Relief for Gay Men by Reconciling the Divided Self

THE DIVIDED SELF AND THE DISEASE OF SECRETS FOR THE GAY AND BISEXUAL MAN

My name is Paul and everyone knows me by this name. If I act in a way that is different from what my upright family, church, and society expect, then I can bring dishonor or disrepute to people in these groups. So, I keep my actions in line with my name and what is expected of me for the sake of approval. I act in ways that are appropriate and my insides and outsides match. But what if I were called Paul day after day but eventually I came to know a new Paul who is gay but who must remain hidden? I know that if this new Paul is discovered, I might bring dishonor to my family, friends, church, and community. I might be alienated or bullied or pushed out of the group.

So, the old Paul becomes a stranger to me while this new Paul is a complete stranger to the outside world, even though I might reveal this identity to a few confidants. The very existence of this new Paul is dangerous, and it is an unstable force since it can bring instant dishonor and even disgrace to the family name and also to those in the community, church, and school. At some point, I may ask myself who is this person who everyone calls Paul. That person is a stranger, and the real Paul—who is gay—is a potential source of instability and danger. I am a stranger to the external world and a danger to my internal self.

Simply put, what if I am something other than the intelligent, rational, clean-cut Boy Scout I thought I was—the one who *was* a good little boy for Mom and Dad? The process of reconciling my true self with who others think I am requires a "breaking down" and a discovering my true identity as a person. (We can and should properly use the word "breakdown" here for lack of a better word.) It is hardly surprising that this "coming out" (or finding out) process is, indeed, messy and is often accompanied by alcohol dependence. My true self needs to be communicated for a unity of the self to be effected.

Why? What if, as a man, I experience lust for a man and conceal this from those around me? What if I am a man married to a woman and I experience lust for another man? Suddenly, there is more to me than what others think and know about me. Should I just try to bury this feeling and repress it as best I can? If I do this, my "self" that I show to the world becomes a caricature—a "cutout" to please family, create a façade, and satisfy society.

So, I create a pretend self that gathers layers of more pretenses and lies until I can't tell the truth from the fiction. There is a split and I become alienated from myself. The public and private are fractured. Who can I blame? I can partially blame an intolerant society for making me this way. I think I have justified anger because I am a hypocrite and a liar and have betrayed what I truly am. Either I did it to myself in order to protect my old self or society did this to me to protect its required sense of order. But someone did something to me that resulted in a betrayal. In this way, the gay or bisexual man becomes a spy in his own land—an alienated self who must not be "found out." Many a gay man feels justified anger at intolerant society for causing him to become a fractured self. Masked anger is a hallmark of gay and bisexual men even though they may not acknowledge it.

If I choose to become an imposter to myself, I am evading growth and creating a lie that splits me. The Canadian psychologist Sidney Jourard made a prescient insight on this subject. He said, My name is an invitation not to change—a command not to change. You still recognize me as this person from yesterday but I know inside that there is now some difference about me. I have discovered something new about myself and now must do everything I can to prevent you from knowing about me."[1]

BECOMING A NEW PERSON

When a gay or bisexual man recognizes certain passions and urges, he knows that he has become a new person. At that point, he needs to make a choice: to convince his family and the community to call him by a new name, or to remain the secretive and angry hypocrite and live a subterranean life. The decision is his. If he chooses the former, this is called growth. He allows another person to know sides of him that are important and new and life-changing. But he also knows there is great danger in doing this. Society, friends, church, and family might not like this new part of him and reject him wholly.

The fundamental fear at work here is the fear of being disowned—of losing the identity he was given by his family, society, and community. As we've already discussed, many gay or bisexual youth are asked to leave their homes because of their orientation. Some religious groups have little or no tolerance for homosexuality. Being rejected from the groups or institutions that made the person who he originally was produces feelings such as 'lost identity' or a fear of "being crazy." This is because my idea of who I am—a social, sexual, and intellectual self—sits squarely in my mind and suddenly I discover that I am something else. This brings confusion, fear, anxiety, and anger—even rage. In many ways, these emotions are the hallmark of many people in the gay community and are a perfect potion for the addictive behavior which is founded on escaping emotions and changing circumstances that the gay or bisexual man finds unacceptable.

Society and the social systems in place have a clear role for me. If I try to change the definition of this slot or this role, I will encounter pressure and threats to keep me frozen and stuck. Things conspire to keep me the way I was yesterday. But today I am an authentic and different person who is capable of new actions and potential. Authentic change requires integrity and that my insides and outside match. Yesterday may have been authentic. But today may be different and also authentic. What do I do with this new sense of world and self and a new authenticity? How do I keep pace? How can I let go of the way I have been? This is very scary. My perceived need to satisfy the objective world keeps me frozen on the outside and alienated on the inside.

My actions no longer satisfy my current needs and my body and my memory. Life is taken from me since I see constant danger in being unmasked. I see life as "going through the motions" to please others and satisfy other people's one-dimensional expectations of me. Yet, my memory and my body experience sex with a man as pleasing and desirable. This in an enlargement. It is real. I can't stop this and the change what is going on. I need to let go of the way I have been. This is terrifying.

Without change, though, I can no longer communicate or live in an authentic way and I cannot interact with others in a way that reflects my growth. Why, then, does the gay or bisexual man remain a spy in his own "country"? If he suddenly lets people know something about him that they never knew before, he may have to pay a high price—retribution from the wife, accusations of being a "fairy" from straight men, discrimination at work. Exclusion, confusion, resentment.[2] This is especially true of deeply religious families or church communities. And this is so true in many cultures throughout Asia.

So the gay or bisexual man conceals it. He stays the original course and invites people to know him as somebody else—as a stranger. In the process, he becomes constrained and alienated from himself. He is forced to fit into a world that is increasingly foreign to him, one that does not fit. His own self is alienated and unnatural—a freak.

The gay or bisexual man's is a case of mistaken identity. People think things about him that are untrue. The way he lets people know things about him is artificial and concocted. It is a wooden life and a divided self. It creates anger and rage because outside conventional thinking has turned him into a fake. This divided man feels like *spoiled goods.*

Of course, there is greater acceptance in the community today when it comes to gay men, lesbians, and bisexuals. Yet there are myriad examples of groups and people who find the gay lifestyle unacceptable. This is certainly true in much of America, as well as in the Far East where I live. In Asia, homosexuality is still something of an anathema and its discovery often brings severe consequences for people, both in their homes and in their places of employment. Many a youth has killed himself or herself over such a discovery. This is not only true in the West but throughout the developing world. Imagine the pressure in China with a one-child policy and a gay male son who is expected to produce a son. Let's not forget that almost eighty countries still see homosexuality as a criminal offense. And several countries still allow a community to kill a man for being gay. One article summed it up well:

> "[Gay and bisexual suicide] attempters reported that they had lost friends because of their disclosures . . . [and] had experienced more victimization and peer rejection based on their sexual orientation."[3]

THE DANGERS OF RESISTING CHANGE

When a man denies change and remains the person society wants him to be, this sets the stage for sickness, neurosis, and denying what is apparent. What satisfied this man before is now boring. Boredom is the best indication of need for change. What was worthwhile before is no longer worthwhile. If a man persists in a way that no longer reflects his newfound sense of the world, he gets sick. He does not grow and instead goes backward. What is the proof that I have not grown when I need to grow? This emotion is boredom.[4]

If I persist in being the person I once was, which I now know is not real or legitimate or authentic, I become neurotic and bored. Something fundamental has changed but I do not. If I pretend to be the person I once was, my actions no longer satisfy a basic human desire for authenticity and integration. I feel bored and lose a sense of motivation. Sickness, demoralization, and a feeling of being dispirited are the natural human result of betraying the true self in such a way. I am dispirited because I am forced to imitate the false person I was yesterday. I have to imitate the person others think I am. This increases the stress in my life and is confusing. I am essentially lost in a series of selves and finally lose sense of which one is the real me. I become self-alienated. After all, what is a breakdown other than a person reaching the limits of his or her existing choices and realizing that none of these choices offer happiness or satisfaction? All of this indeed sets the stage for a breakdown. It is probably necessary, as I need to break out—not break down.

Some resolution of this broken or fractured self is required or I will want to keep anesthetizing myself—with alcohol, drugs, sex, work, gambling, money. This is a perfectly natural response to denial and the creation of multiple false selves.

HOW TO INITIATE CHANGE

I am only a once born person. I need to be twice born.

I need to change, not check out. I want to leave my body. I want to change my emotional response to a situation that I find unacceptable. I outgrow my identity but I am terrified of change because it involves the dissolution of the person I have spent years creating.

How do I change from this Hell of an alienated self? Meditation and honest reflection on my experience is a good starting point. Look at what is in front of you. What is my path? What is my role? What is my identity?

I need to disengage and become unhypnotized and see myself in a way that can allow myself to emerge in a new light.

We need an odyssey of change with a vision, an ideal, and heroes. Here are a few touchstones to initiate change.

1. Gather the imagination to consider other things when the old way becomes stale. Consider:
   - What if it is okay to be gay? What would life be like if others accepted me as a gay man?
   - What if I found a church that especially welcomed me because I am a gay man?
   - What if I could find reconciliation with my wife as a bisexual man?
2. Consider the status quo and what the world is like if we change.
   - What if I could love myself as a gay man for the first time?
   - What would it be like if I could tell my parents and friends that I am gay and proud?
   - What if I just did not care if a religious group told me I was damned for being gay?

3. Disengage to consider change. Drugs and honesty are polar opposites.
   - What if I did not need to use drugs and alcohol to hook up with men?
   - What if I could be a gay man and also be clean and sober?
   - What would it feel like to have sober sex with another man I cared about?
4. Gather the courage and resolve to let go and tolerate being nowhere for a while.
   - What if I gave myself permission to disengage from work for a while to heal?
   - What if I could try to jettison those feelings and thoughts that being gay is bad?
   - What if I could remove all that heavy armor I have put on myself to protect myself?
5. Envision another way. Gather the resolve to dive back in and improve a situation.
   - What if I could forgive myself for being sexually abused as a child?
   - What if I could forgive my abuser and finally move on with my life as a responsible adult?
   - What if I could forgive adults for creating an unsafe environment for me as a child?
6. Try to think of changing with no guarantee that the first attempt will work.
   - What if I told my parents I was gay or lesbian and they rejected me? Can I still be okay?
   - What if an abuser refused to acknowledge something happened? Can I be okay?
   - What if a parent said, "I did the best I could, so drop it." Can I be okay with this?
7. Think about how much people do NOT want us to change. This is difficult.
   - Have I considered how much my father would want a straight son?
   - Have I considered that men who reject my being gay are fearful of hidden gay feelings themselves?
   - Have I considered a mother who may love me deeply and is merely concerned about HIV?
8. Think about life having a meaning built on health, liberation, serenity, and happiness.
   - If I could describe a happy life, what would it be?
   - If I could describe a life of liberation, what would it be?
   - If I could describe a live with peace of mind, what would it be?

9. Think about what limits me. Press against these limits gently.
   - What limits on my sexuality are there *today* that I can change?
   - What limits are there *today* on my fear of past emotions that limit me?
   - What limits are there *today* on trying to forgive an adult who abused me in the present day?

10. Think about what truthful dialogue is. Unashamed open disclosure is healthy. We discover limits by doing this.[5]
    - What secret would I tell today if I had a friend who would love me no matter what?
    - What would I say to an abuser if that abuser was sitting in a chair in front of me?
    - Did I go back for more of the sexual abuse because I liked it?

If the way I am in the world makes me bored or sick or if I find my actions sickening, I must then push against the limits of growth. Men have a natural desire to explore. Boredom is an excellent indication that new exploration is necessary. I need to move my body anew. I need to remove the armor. An unwillingness to grow and explore leads to feelings of being uptight, angry, and repressed. Acknowledgment, talking about events, reflecting about the events and some form of forgiveness is required. For that is human nature. Otherwise, we cannot move on. The rattling boxes in the attic must be brought down at some point. When they are brought down and when we open them, 95 percent of the time they are harmless. We just allow the ghosts in the attic to grow and fester. Confronting the truth of our past offers liberation to move on with the trudge of life. Forgiveness offers a way out and a means of flying to new heights.

NOTES

1. Sidney Jourard, Lecture, Florida Presbyterian College, September 27, 1969.
2. Ibid.
3. S. L. Hershberger, N. W. Pilkington, and A. R. D'Augelli, "Predictors of Suicide Attempts among Gay, Lesbian, and Bisexual Youth," *Journal of Adolescent Research* 12 no. 4 (Oct. 1997): 477–97.
4. Sidney Jourard lecture. Op cit. It is a terrible tragedy that Jourard died in a freak accident in his garage while working on a car. His insights were profound.
5. Some of this language is drawn from an assortment of Jourard lectures prior to his death.

Chapter Seven

The Social Spirituality vs. Science

Why Should We Remain Hopeful

Many gay and bisexual men wonder if it is worth it to continue with life. One study of almost 35,000 gay men found far higher rates of generalized anxiety, mood disorders, and alcoholism in states that still banned gay marriage compared to those that legalized marriage.[1] In another recent study of gay men, bisexuals, and lesbians, as many as one-third of participants had attempted suicide.[2] And in a 2011 study of 32,000 young people age sixteen to seventeen, one in five of those who identified themselves as gay, bisexual, or lesbian reported having attempted suicide with the most common reason being that he or she was in an unsupportive environment. This is five times the rate of suicide attempts in the general heterosexual population.[3]

How can the gay and bisexual community overcome and thrive amid the discrimination, bullying, ignorance, prejudice, and stigma that remains with us even despite our progress? How can gay and bisexual men find a path in life that offers peace of mind and some form of happiness when they face such high odds of addiction, mental disorders, rejection, and social harassment? The alternative question is how can we reduce the rate of suicidality in the gay community? In this chapter, we will explore ways that gay and bisexual men can embark on a spiritual path to resilience and hope even while enduring begrudging tolerance or outright expulsion from church or the spiritual community.

AN ATTITUDE OF HOPE

Let's step back and consider two of the most revered figures on resilience in the twentieth century. One was a survivor of a death camp during World War II whose mother, sister, and wife were murdered by the Nazis. Another was one of the most famous psychologists in America who lived a life of melancholy and depression and who lost a sister to mental illness and a brother to alcoholism. One was Protestant, the other Jewish. Both men were extraordinarily talented medical doctors and psychiatrists who treated mental disorders. At some point, they both asked whether there is an important passive element to the phenomenon of personal redemption or resilience. They ask whether there is a non-human support or a kind of zeitgeist or inner self that we fall back on during moments of self-despair or times when suicide seems a viable way out.

Viktor Frankl wrote *Man's Search for Himself* (1945) in a few weeks. William James's *Varieties of Religious Experience* (1902) was transcribed from a series of lectures over a few weeks in Edinburgh, Scotland.[4] Both books became international best sellers; both touched on the issue of addiction and attempted to answer the riddle of how humans cope and find meaning in the face of overwhelming physical and mental suffering. And, though the two books both come to a spiritual answer to the bewildering riddle of human suffering, they do so in very different ways.

They both ask why some people choose or adopt an attitude of hope rather than an attitude of resignation in the face of alienation, hopelessness, and fear. Are some simply predisposed to having an attitude of hope? If so, how does it surface from underneath a mountain of self-despair? Most important, both ask how it is possible that people with a deep and beautiful sense of hope had at earlier points in their lives experienced profound and degrading suffering.

The other side of the question, which is the all-important practical part, is this: Who are these people who create and sustain hope, and how do we imitate them? Both of these doctors focused on the kind of people who have known profound suffering and yet managed to develop an attitude of hope that provides a sense of responsibility to engage in altruistic action to help others. Interestingly, both focus on how they believe this process works in addiction.

Frankl wrote about suffering that was imposed from the outside—his experiences in a Nazi concentration camp where only three in one hundred made it out alive. The rest were starved, beaten to death, or gassed. James wrote about self-imposed suffering of the "diseased" sick soul (and very often these are alcoholics) and made reference to his own struggle with lifelong feelings of melancholy and alienation. Frankl's physical prison at Auschwitz was one of indescribable cruelty. The prison described by James, on the other hand, was figurative but reveals how a sick soul may be imprisoned by suffering, fear, depression, and worthlessness seemingly for his entire life.

Frankl was asking the following question: how do I create meaning in my life in a world that seems arbitrary, cruel, and diseased? James was asking a similar question: how can dying and hopeless drunks in their self-constructed prisons of addiction somehow gain a sense of hope and a changed attitude after a lifetime of defeat, alienation, depression, and self-loathing?

They both want to know how the suffering of the soul (the inner self or higher self) can be alleviated, expiated, or expunged. That is, they both want to unlock the secret of this eternal mystery called human redemption. (Redemption is the act of salvation to change, and resilience is the act of a healthy attitude toward life and a willingness to help others.)

Sick souls, James says, are that way not because of anything they have actually experienced. The suffering of the sick soul is characterized by lifelong depression, anxiety, fear, self-pity, and a sense of hopelessness. He calls their lives a "series of zig-zaps."[5] These sick souls appear to have a heightened sensitivity to their own suffering as well as the suffering of others. They seem to have extra antennae to the suffering of the world and cannot pass by it without staring in morbid fascination. The sick soul with a hypersensitivity to suffering seems to stew in his suffering and any other suffering that is loitering about. They are essentially "diseased" by this sensitivity to suffering.

James distinguishes these sick souls from healthy-minded people who are capable of casting their gaze away from evil and suffering and moving on with life. Those who are happy-minded seem to have an "innate optimism." They love, sin, confess, trust, laugh, and move on. James offers the amusing quote that happy-minded people "seem to be born with an extra bottle of champagne to their credit." He says they seem to have born this way.[6]

In his description of these "diseased souls," he presents the same conclusion as Frankl: Those who have endured much lifelong suffering are the ones who come out transformed (redeemed?) and are all the better for it. They are somehow more worthy, more free, and more complete. In either case, both men fundamentally believed that suffering was somehow necessary to be complete, as long as it was "necessary" suffering and not concocted for its own sake. The question is how can a person experiencing pitiful and lasting suffering be pulled back from the gates of death when it makes logical sense to commit suicide? The answers of James and Frankl have everything to do with their own internal makeup.

Both men use the phrase "inner self" (James also calls it the "better self" or "higher self") to describe that entity we access when we leave a conscious self wrapped up and overcome with suffering. This is especially true for the drug addict. In this inner self lies hope and salvation.

How we get to this higher self or higher power is the question of the ages. In Frankl's case, there are two stages, but he essentially says it is a decision.

The first is the recognition of nakedness—our "naked existence" is shown to us through experiences of suffering. After this comes the second phase, which Frankl called apathy. James called it "self-surrender in a moment of self-despair." Disgust, horror, and pity vanish. Frankl has the brilliant phrase to explain this: An abnormal reaction to abnormal circumstances is normal. This apathy in the midst of constant suffering as well as physical and mental torture is almost normal, natural, and expected. It is a human reaction to attend only to the basic instincts in the face of extreme danger. It should result in giving up. James came to the same conclusion. Both agree that self-surrender in a moment of self-despair and apathy is absolutely human. And this is the beginning of redemption.

Frankl says many times that one attaches himself to an attitude of hope in order to remain sane and detached from the animal cruelty and suffering. One makes a decision and reaches out for it—*he somehow arranges a meeting with it.* Frankl says in his own case that it was always there. He says his "inner self" that showed the way was his own intellectual life and the memory of his wife. He says the memories of his own "rich intellectual life" and the "loving contemplation" of the memory of his wife presented themselves and caused the positive shift in attitude toward the arbitrary cruelty before him. This somehow made it bearable *for him* and gave meaning to *his* suffering. His rich memories and intellectual interior were of no comfort to anyone else around him.

James uses surprisingly similar language and says that we and this higher power have business with each other. He refers to this higher power or higher self as a serious higher power (he also calls it "a god" on occasion) who can deal with us in the gravest of times on the retail level—the level of the personal. It is not a wholesale god who is detached from life. The childish gods we grew up with need to be swept away in favor of a power who can offer hope and strength amid a deep life crisis. When the half-gods go, the real gods arrive. This is his rallying point.

Frankl says that a sense of hope comes from surrender. This sense of hope also brings with it the strength to reach out and ask for help, for that was what his discovered (chosen?) attitude of love demanded of him. With a newfound attitude of hope and peace comes a sense of responsibility to do something about one's situation. He is clear that this is *his* experience and how he was able to reach within *himself* and find that inner self or "inner optimism." This is his own personal journey. James has the same conclusion and says that this journey is always deeply personal and is barely known and understood by the person experiencing the process of redemption.

SACRED CAULDRONS: REINTRODUCING SPIRITUALITY TO PSYCHOTHERAPISTS' OFFICES

Lionel Corbett may be onto something when he says there is great meaning behind suffering that goes far beyond the current models of treatment. The results from treating emotional problems with psycho-dynamic psychotherapy are only moderately good.[1] The results are also mixed for cognitive-behavioral or pharmacological approaches.[2] His bottom line is that we are limiting ourselves "if we see emotional distress as nothing more than a brain problem or the result of learned cognitive distortions. This is a subtle cultural promotion of materialism which ignores the spiritual dimension of the personality."

As with Frankl and James, Corbett concludes that incorporating a personal spirituality into treatment can make an important contribution. After all, what is spirituality, William James says, but man's response to life that can offer enchantment, a sense of safety and connection, and a sense of heroism.

Spirituality is not religion and never has been. These are two different realms and a spiritual experience preceded religion—not the other way around. Spirituality arises organically from the depth of one's being and is truly authentic. Doctors and therapists need not be embarrassed if they admit they have a spiritual life. The individual's life is a complex web of dreams, complexes, and suffering. It is a sacred text. This spiritual experience is mediated by the unconscious, a fact that William James first pointed out, so a deep psychological approach to spirituality is logical. Corbett concludes: "The distinction between spirituality and psychology is as arbitrary as a line on a map dividing two countries."[3]

Notes

1. Roseborough, 2006.
2. Walsh, et al., 2002.
3. Lionel Corbett, *Sacred Cauldron,* chapter 2, Chiron, 2011.

AN ATTITUDE OF LOVE

Frankl says that memories of loved ones amid the suffering transform the suffering and create a loving attitude of action. This freedom to choose an attitude of love (he calls it an "inner decision") of mankind—the last thing man has as a free being—leads to the responsibility of right action and service.

Thinking of others is the only way out, argues Frankl. He makes the beautiful point that creature comforts for our little selves only make us more unhappy. This inner self that gives meaning to suffering and causes us to be of service is precisely anchored in "spiritual things." This is the "why" to live for—this inner self of memories, images, and love.

James comes to the same conclusion but says that the process of purging the ancient sins and asking for forgiveness strengthen and sustain this process of redemption. The resilience to sustain a healthy attitude in life comes from seeking forgiveness and engaging in service. Indeed, the resilience for James comes only from service. Without service and action, the process of redemption dies off. A newfound spiritual life must be nurtured or it wilts on the vine. Frankl does not talk much about the process of forgiving his oppressors.

It is easy for a man like Frankl to call up glorious memories of love and great accomplishment. Before he entered the death camp, he was accomplished, highly intelligent, innately optimistic, and not infected with the soul sickness so beautifully detailed by James in *Varieties*. The soul sickness of the man overwhelmed by a sense of isolation and rottenness annihilates the good and creates a universe of alienation for the interior life of the sick-souled person. He does *not* create a life worthy of beautiful memories and loving relationships. He can't seem to. Rather, he creates a life of depression, anxiety, and alienation because that is what he knows. The sick soul (James points out that so many of these cases are alcoholics and used the language of the time by referring to them as "drunkards") just does not have access to that reservoir of memories. It is a dry riverbed. Sick souls just do not have that capacity for calling up memories, for any good memories (if there are any left) are washed away by a torrent of alienation and depression.

This soul-sick alcoholic must be offered some aid, either by the subconscious or "from above." One is natural and the other is supernatural. The sick soul is too "choked up with evil" to consciously and willingly tap into that inner or higher self of his own volition. The sick-souled person must be given a second chance. James refers to it as "twice born optimism." In any event, this psychic change must burst forth from within not as a decision but as a desperate gasp of the exhausted man who does not decide—he surrenders! James makes it clear it does not matter how it happens. Whether it is a "psychic lesion bursting forth" from the unconscious or "a mystical touch of grace" that (inexplicably) also seems to come to us from the unconscious, it does not matter. What is important is only that it happens and the fruits of the experience.

James comes to the precise conclusion as Frankl, stating that the end of suffering is loving gratefulness and an attitude of service to others. Both agree that humans are somehow cleansed by suffering and both believe that the product of this bursting through of the inner self is a life of service to others.

WILLIAM JAMES'S SIBLINGS: ONE GAY, ONE ALCOHOLIC, ONE FINANCIAL FAILURE, ONE MENTALLY ILL

William James had his hands full with his family. Even though he was born into a very wealthy "Boston Brahmin" family of great prestige, his siblings had a tough time of it. His youngest brother was named Robertton (Bob) and he lived in the home of William James as he was drinking himself to death. He eventually died of alcoholism. His brother Garth was plagued with ill health and bad business decisions and died at thirty-eight of kidney failure. His younger sister Alice was mentally ill and housebound for most of her life with "neuralgia" of "extreme anxiety." She tragically died of breast cancer at forty-two. Only Henry seemed to have a happy life as one of the most famous American authors, whose novels include *The American* and *The Turn of the Screw*. Henry never married and is thought to have been gay. His personal letters show homoerotic emotions and veiled eroticism for, among others, a twenty-seven-year-old sculptor named Hendrik Anderson. Despite the plight of his siblings—mental illness, financial failure, alcoholism—William went on to become the Father of American Psychology and his gay brother, Henry, is celebrated as one of the greatest American novelists of the late 1800s and early 1900s. We don't get to choose our families. But we can choose our path.

SELF-SURRENDER

How do humans gain distance from an overwhelming feeling that life is nothing but rottenness? Sick-souled alcoholics see the skull grinning at any banquet they attend. Life for them is a cruel joke. They require a "twice born optimism" through a psychic change to appreciate the grandness and felicity of life.

How can a man engulfed in suffering find the means through an inner decision to gain distance and rise above it? Indeed, there is *no inner decision at all*. The man must not decide—he must surrender to his shams and realize his own nakedness and apathy. As with Frankl, he surrenders in a state of total ridiculous nakedness. There must be, for both James and Frankl, an emotional death. This decision to surrender comes from a realization deep in the soul that we are all made of the same clay. We are one with the criminal, the insane, the doctor, and the composer. A fundamental feeling of oneness in this fleshly existence is the key starting point. From this moment of emotional death comes a feeling of democracy and sameness and belonging. The same redemption comes to one and all no matter what.

James said an abandonment of a lower self (Frankl's notion of self-detachment and union with the inner self) is necessary to make any sense of suffering. The sick soul must experience a self-surrender through self-despair in order to rise above his convulsive little self. An inner decision and reliance on memories and images is futile, since the "inward pollution" clouds all emotions and feelings.

Here we use the wonderful analogy of Frankl's interior canister. Frankl suggests that the shame, guilt, or self-loathing of each person is a cancerous vapor that fills up the entire interior canister in its entirety. No matter how little or how much shame and guilt each person has, the contents of the canister are *completely* filled and the person is overcome with the noxious gases of doubt, remorse, and self-loathing. The size of human suffering—and the ancient sins to be overcome—is absolutely relative to each other. It is overwhelming for each person and each feels the same disgust and self-pity in their own way.

James would be in utter agreement with this and would clearly say those engulfed with their own suffering and the suffering of those around them do not stand a chance in making that inner decision. The sick soul has a diseased hypersensitivity that allows in all the suffering that can fit, drowning a person in grief and brokenheartedness. (Is this unnecessary suffering, he asks? NO! It is what it is!)

For James, the decision to make meaning of life must come from outside the conscious self. The higher self somehow reaches for the known or lower self. We reach for it as it is reaching for us. It is done through a passive experience. It is not a leap into faith but rather a retreat into faith. The psychic change is a passive effort when it comes to spirituality. James says "hands off." He surmised that this change somehow incubates in the subconscious and seems to burst forth unaided. Natural or supernatural, it is a passive action that the person allows to happen.

For Frankl, change comes from a decision to reach for that higher self. He makes it very clear that we can choose to fill the interior canister with either joy *or* suffering. The choice is ours.

For James, the exhausted brain center of the sick soul (let us call it the addict) just goes on strike in a spiritual experience of psychic conversion and a higher power seems to take over. Call it the subconscious, if you wish. For James, it is more of a passive affair while for Frankl, it is an active affair. But the result of making contact with this inner self or higher self create a different attitude and outlook on life, which offers hope and strength to carry on and change.

What about the needless suffering people endure? Frankl sees sin or suffering as a "crime" of civilization. Both he and James conclude that a person can make a decision to call up his better angels (or attitudes) by a process of self-detachment from worldly goods. For James, it is a practical necessity for

FINDING A HIGHER SELF AS MY LOWER SELF IS FALLING TO PIECES

William James says that a spiritual experience is a "falling back" process and not a "jumping onto" process. We fall back into a high self that has been there along just as out smaller self is dying and falling away. This self-surrender is a dying process and he connects this to the process of sobriety for alcoholics and drug addicts. In this way, it is definitely a grieving process not unlike Elizabeth Kubler-Ross's Five Stages. Denial is the first step of knowing there is a reality of a better self we are not ready to accept. Denial buys time when we are not ready to accept a new reality.

The second phase is when reality enters. Anger is about an inability to control anything. This goes for the soldier in the field who loses a good friend, a young man who loses his father to alcoholism or a 40 year old man who loses his career through drug addiction. This is rage at a universe which spins in its own time without any help from us. The third is sorrow and this comes from the dam of tears which burst forth after the shams are over, the wounds are opened and reality has begun. A man need not smear himself all over with a hypocritical show of virtue. The gift of tears comes forth.

The fourth is the bargain which says, 'Now that my problems are shown forth, maybe I can have a drink or two. I am better now, aren't I? It is a healthy response and guards against a reality for which we are not quite ready. This is the source of relapse even after great progress with therapy, twelve step action or self-help.

The fifth is all about acceptance which is full and complete. It is about recognition of total powerlessness. There is great fear here but great freedom when the weight is lifted and we realize we are responsible for this one—our attitude. It is pure honesty about our state in the universe. Margaret Fuller said, "I accept the universe." Thomas Carlyle said in return, "Egad, she'd better." This is good advice for all of us!

The works of Frankl, James, Kubler-Ross and Bill Wilson are surprisingly similar. Recognition of powerlessness, falling back on some better self, feeling sorrow for past damage done by us or to us and accepting the world as it is creates a spiritual experience which offers peace of mind in a seemingly uncaring universe which is spinning all on its own.

people to experience a sort of redemption in order to escape the problem of addiction, which he said was genetic (decades ahead of his time). The alienated sick soul needs subconscious support to bring about a psychic change in a moment of self-despair and lifelong suffering. This requires surrendering to a higher self or a higher power through an experience of self-despair. This allows the person to build a meaningful life, of which service to others is the new foundation. Redemption through surrender in a crisis of self-despair brings equality, democracy, confession, humility, and right action—and gratitude! This, in turn, leads to happiness and peace of mind. Resilience in the face of failure, rejection, and arbitrary disaster can remain as long as service to others and a cultivation of some spiritual life is maintained. For both James and Frankl, a spiritual life without action is empty talk and a waste of time.

The people we most admire are those who have endured extreme heartache and suffering and yet contribute so much to human life culture by healing, laughing, helping, and offering comfort. Was the suffering worth it? Was it necessary? James refers us to the story of Job in the Old Testament, which is the ageless story of the necessity of suffering. The problem is that if God can prevent suffering and chooses not to, he is malevolent. If God cannot prevent suffering but claims he is omnipotent, then he is incompetent and a liar. Either way, there is the problem of suffering. On this argument, James says that all the books that try to understand this problem of suffering and evil (and a God who either is unwilling or unable to help) should be committed to flames if the outcome does not result in right action to be of service to others. It is not anti-intellectual. It is pragmatic. We pitch in, he says, and (who knows) maybe we tilt the bar a little in favor of goodness. Maybe, he says, we can even give this higher power a hand to fight the good fight. For both men, forgiveness is the key. Without forgiveness, there is no way out.

In the end, both conclude that finding hope through some appeal to an inner source of strength as we detach from unimportant external conditions in the here and now is the key. James and Frankl agree that the freedom to choose a healthy-minded attitude is all a man has. Is the attitude of gratitude a "free gift of grace" or "payment for hours worked"? James believes the former, but says that active service to sustain the experience of gratitude creates the resilience to endure and maintain hope.

Frankl says the same thing. They agree that the debate is not about who is right and wrong and why there is good and evil. They both argue that liberation from a life of suffering must result in filial love as well as forgiveness and not anger, vengeance, excess, or fanaticism. They also agree that the only avenue to redemption is ultimately through forgiveness. It must be a life where expectations are dashed and we learn to cultivate an attitude of service for its own sake.

ADVICE FROM VIKTOR FRANKL AND WILLIAM JAMES: WHAT TO DO WHEN YOU ARE WALKING THROUGH HELL

1. There is no way to escape suffering in life. It is part of the human story. We receive external suffering from people who are homophobes, mon-

sters, or mentally ill. Many of us have internal suffering in the form of inner struggles such as alcoholism and mental disorders, which create barriers to happiness and peace of mind. Accepting this fact of suffering is the key to getting better. Naming the various types of suffering creates hope, since getting a diagnosis is the starting point to treatment and healing. Alcoholism is a disease and needs to be treated with biological, psychological, and social means. Being gay or bisexual is *not* a disease and does not require a treatment. Many consider it a gift and something to be embraced and cherished. We have many gay heroes.

2. Many gay and bisexual men have encountered distant fathers, cool receptions by churches, discrimination, beatings, bullying, verbal abuse, and stigmatization as they grew into manhood. They lived highly stressful double lives. Viktor Frankl said that an abnormal reaction to an abnormal circumstance is normal. Many gay and bisexual men escape this unpleasantness through drugs and alcohol. Gay and bisexual men in recovery can forgive themselves for escaping into addiction since it seemed, at first, a perfectly good idea. It was an abnormal response to an abnormal circumstance. Forgiveness of self is necessary here.
3. Self-despair is a moment when even disgust, self-pity, and rage no longer have any meaning. From this comes a natural human response, which is an emotional death. We lose the will to live and a self-surrender is the result. We do not make a leap to some kind of faith, but rather seem to fall back on some inner self, higher self, or higher power. This occurs in a state of emotional nakedness. It is utterly personal and non-religious. The religion comes much later. The gay man on his last hit of crystal meth will often feel this way. His moral death is his spiritual birthday.
4. Frankl said we need to arrange a meeting with this inner self. James concurs that we and this higher power have serious business with each other. Both men are clear that the extreme nature of the circumstance requires a higher power who is not a childish puritanical god with a bleak and chalky outlook. It is an emotional experience that can be built on loving memories, humor, curiosity, or natural beauty. It is an experience in which the old ideas of a half-god must be dropped in favor of one's own idea of a powerful figure. Both are unequivocal in their experience: if we reach for this inner self, it will reach back as a source of strength.
5. This reaching out to an inner self or a higher self has a feeling of detachment to it. It has a feeling of becoming objective from physical objects. This does not mean that we recklessly pursue poverty, but rather than we gain the emotional freedom to pursue a more spiritual path where priorities change and where the source of happiness moves from physical things to personal things.

6. James goes down the path of looking at religions over the centuries and notes that the expiation of ancient sins is needed. Shams are over. The light is required and old bandages to cover old sores must be removed for healing to occur. Forgiveness is sought and often a damn of tears is opened to cleanse away the ancient sins. This confession of sins and request for forgiveness creates a feeling of belonging and a sense of a wider life.
7. Many things can sustain these experiences. Loving memories of past family members or friends can help. Having a sense of humor seems to be a key element. According to James, unnecessary suffering or morbid religious practices where privation, pain, or harsh discipline are common is not the proper fruit of a spiritual experience. Joy and serenity are the proper outcomes of a spiritual experience—not pain and suffering. The gay community needs to be more aggressive in creating and honoring heroes. It must honor gay people not because of how they died but because of how they lived. Men like Tennessee Williams and Truman Capote gave us some of the finest literature of the twentieth century. Freddy Mercury gave us some of the finest rock music. Their causes of death should be less important than what they brought to life.
8. This experience of hope and serenity is helped along only by helping others who cannot take care of themselves. Reaching out in volunteerism is a vital way to maintain resilience and hope in the face of suffering. Frankl and James are unequivocal on this. Helping others is the way out of hell. The more we help, the more strength we get. This is one of the core paradoxes of spirituality over the past five thousand years in every religious practice. In this spiritual world, which is increasingly divorced from physical things, I discover the reason to the question "Why do I live?" It is to help others.
9. In hindsight, we have a new sense of the suffering that was part of our lives in the past, especially for those in addiction. It was for a purpose and that purpose was to reach a point where the addict could be of service. The past suffering makes sense in the context of service. In a way, the suffering is made legitimate.
10. The underlying assumption in all this—and the easy transition to help those in need, whether they are homeless or crazy—is that we know that we are all made of the same clay. Whether we are robber, doctor, lunatic, or composer, we are all one. We all come from the same source and we are united by this source. There is great comfort in this and it is easy to forgive people when we realize that we are all made of flesh and blood.
11. The shame, guilt, and self-loathing that each man carries around with him fits like a vapor in his *own self*. No matter what we have all done, we all have an overwhelming need to expiate the wrongs of the past, forgive

ourselves, and move on with service to others. We each experience suffering that feels overwhelming to us. William James says that the sick-souled alcoholic is filled with this from the get-go regardless of actions. No matter what the source of the activity or the failure, the sources of that suffering must be respected and dealt with honorably no matter how great or small. We all have a story which is our story. And this story must be told. The truth demands a voice. A wise man once said that if we could all throw our problems in a pile and pick anyone else's problems, we would always retrieve our own.

12. For Frankl and James, the ultimate choice is about the attitude we have when we are connected to this inner or higher self. We can choose to have an attitude of hope and salvation or an attitude of darkness. This is the ultimate freedom. A spiritual path helps in choosing a hopeful attitude, James asserts. While the path does not need to be spiritual, it helps if it is. This path of a positive attitude brings peace of mind, a sense of belonging, a sense that there is something wider than me and an obligation to be of service. Frankl did not know James; he lived in a different time, in a different religion and culture, and yet he arrived at the identical conclusion.

We must all do this alone but we do it together. Each man must meet this inner self or higher self (or higher power of the "maker") by himself in all his nakedness. It is a feeling of falling back into the arms of something greater than me. Mankind has been writing about this phenomenon for five thousand years, so whatever is here is persistent, repeatable, and palpable. Achieving a naked honesty and realizing that we are all in the same predicament creates a new source of strength and a new attitude toward the fact of suffering. In our aloneness is found the strength to endure and not to annihilate ourselves.

RESILIENCE

The real title of Frankl's book, which he wrote after he left Auschwitz and after he knew his mother, brother, and wife were murdered, is *Say Yes to Life in Spite of Everything.* That is resilience. It is the freedom to be alone in all my moral and emotional nakedness standing in front of my Maker. It is then that I am given the strength to realize that life is not about comfort but about service. In that nakedness is a connection to strength that endures all suffering.

In conclusion, specialists like Paul Kwon at Washington State University are doing very specific work in the area of resilience in the gay and bisexual community, especially concerning factors of social support and acceptance from the community, church, and family. Without a dramatic change from the community, the world of the gay or bisexual man is perilous. Indeed, there is a litany of data in this book that reveals how the gay and bisexual man *still* has appalling outcomes due to a lack of acceptance in the community. Social support allows gay and bisexual men to be true to themselves and not live in a divided self, which is full of shame, guilt, and self-loathing.

The result of this is less prejudice and stigmatization, which causes isolation, loneliness, and a disenfranchisement from society. This is true with ethnic minorities, but is especially true for those whose sexual orientation is not just sneered at by many, but for which people can be imprisoned, fired from their jobs, or ostracized from society in some countries—still! Acceptance and integration can lead to an ability to offer help in the developmental needs of the gay and bisexual community. This is a community that is still, I strongly believe, traumatized by the wipeout of a vast swath of the gay community in the 1980s and 1990s from AIDS. Another friend who was a professional choreographer in the 1980s (and who lives with HIV) told me that both of the original dance troupe of the hit musical *Cats* (premiering in 1981) was virtually wiped out by AIDS by 1995.

Furthermore, Kwon believes there is a need to allow the gay and bisexual community to process emotions—PTSD from the AIDS scourge of the 1980s and 1990s, for instance—in an insightful manner to reduce the negative impact of prejudice and stigmatization. Insightful processing of emotions may sound corny, but it is a vital part of rejuvenating a community that still has appalling rates of addiction. We have come very far, but we have so far to go.

With hope and optimism, gay and bisexual men can maintain psychological health in the face of ongoing prejudice. Achieving the milestones is also helpful: One milestone is the processing of the pain and anguish of the death and sickness of AIDS and HIV. Alan Downes, author of *The Velvet Rage,* is onto something very powerful about the ongoing mass PTSD in the gay community. I covered this in a precious chapter, but the community should accept the challenge of treating the "stigma of the dying and the diseased" carried by so many gay and bisexual men. The stories about the cast of *Cats* offer powerful anecdotal evidence. To hear these stories in 2014 causes an all-too-familiar sadness that collects over the years like barnacles on the bottom of a ship. Another milestone which is controversial and a vital part of mental health involves making decisions to maintain physical and mental health. When gay can face the future armed with knowledge about options and outcomes of sexual behavior that shuns risky sex without offending those who are currently HIV-positive. I absolutely believe there is no conflict in creating simple, sincere, and forceful messages to encourage safer sex for all while also encouraging those who live with HIV to reject prejudice and stigma. A third milestone is when they can embrace their own community of gay and bisexual heroes and look at the phenomenal pool of talent and contribution to western culture, regardless of how these people died (I have launched a nonprofit organization that celebrates the gay heroes of western civilization; see the website www.rainbowwarriors.me.

A fourth milestone of progress is that gay men can feel safe to engage in the workplace without fear of prejudice or discrimination. Similarly, progress occurs when gay men can take advantage of public services and job programs that build self-esteem and create economic opportunities for a group of people who are overwhelmingly law-abiding citizens who offer a great deal to society. (The website www.crystalmeth.org is a great source for public information and guidance for addicts).[7]

I know a gay couple who live active and vibrant lives. Both of them are terrific teachers who have won awards. Both teach in an elite private school in a city in Asia but must live in different cities to avoid attracting attention. It is clear that they would be fired if their sexual orientation became public. This is all common in too many cities. The inference is that if two men live together, they are living in a kind of criminal relationship. Even though they are both pillars of the community, they live in fear of a "knock on the door" one day when it will all suddenly be over. This is no way to live. It leads to a quiet kind of self-loathing, a slow burn to resignation and surrender to "the fates," and creates a chronically distressing undertow to the relationship. Again, we have come so far, but there is do much farther to go.

NOTES

1. Mark L. Hatzenbuehler, MS, MPhil, Katie A. McLaughlin, PhD, Katherine M. Keyes, MPH, and Deborah S. Hasin, PhD, "The Impact of Institutional Discrimination on Psychiatric Disorders in Lesbian, Gay, and Bisexual Populations: A Prospective Study." AJPH, March 2010, p 452–459.
2. Brian S. Mustanski, PhD, Robert Garofalo, MD, MPH, and Erin M. Emerson, MA. "Mental Health Disorders, Psychological Distress, and Suicidality in a Diverse Sample of Lesbian, Gay, Bisexual, and Transgender Youths." AJPH, December 2010, Vol. 100, pp. 2426–32.
3. Mark L. Hatzenbuehler, PhD, The Social Environment and Suicide Attempts in Lesbian, Gay, and Bisexual Youth. Pediatrics, online publication April 18, 2011.
4. James, op.cit. And Frankl, Viktor, "Man's Search for Meaning." Beacon Press, 1956. (This was the first translation into English. It was originally published in 1946 as Ein Psycholog erlebt das Konzentrationslager). Frankl wrote it in two weeks.
5. For further detail on how James describes the life of the alcoholic as a sick soul who is seeking an exit from a prison of fear, anxiety and self-loathing, see my book "Cravings for Deliverance." Lantern press, 2014.
6. Schulte, *Cravings for Deliverance,* op cit.
7. Paul Kwon, Washington State University, GLBT resilience find reference.

Part Three

THE CONTROVERSIES AND CONTRADICTIONS IN RECOVERY

Chapter Eight

Disease, Disorder, and the Disorders

What's the Difference?

> In the Jungian tradition, our psychology cannot be radically separated from our spirituality, because the human personality has an archetypal or spiritual foundation as well as its developmental and human aspects. The therapeutic approach should not try to compete with the spiritual but it can offer an alternative approach to suffering.
>
> —Lionel Corbett, *The Sacred Cauldron*

MISPERCEPTIONS

Behavioral disorders arise from skewed perception about the outside world. This skewed perception can stem from a strongly perceived but incorrect sense of imminent danger, which makes for fearful responses to normal stimuli. People with substance abuse issues often say this is a key emotion running through their minds. What came first—the substance or the feeling of danger? Secondly, these disorders arise from a sense of a foreshortened life regardless of outside evidence, which makes for panicky or irrational behavior. People with substance abuse issues also comment about a sense of doom or foreshortened life. What came first—the substance or the sense of imminent doom? Thirdly, this skewed perception arises from a fear of rejection from a loved one without any evidence to the contrary, which makes for irritating overcompensation of bossiness. What came first—the substance or the fear of rejection? Or this skewed perception can arise from an emotional insecurity arising from a feeling of being unworthy, broken, fraudulent, or a phony, which makes for being a doormat, a wilting violet, or wallflower and letting people walk over them. This is heard quite often in the rooms of

Alcoholics Anonymous. The alcoholic often feels like he or she is unfinished, broken, or was a "lemon" from the very start.

These fears are irrational to the outside world but have an appalling air of certainty to the individual experiencing them. For people with behavioral disorders, the filter that should process incoming data from the outside world seems to be broken or impaired. The false or faulty information they take in leads them to react in bizarre or inappropriate ways. It is almost a kind of emotional autism. Mountains of emotional waves—some correct, others incorrect or incoherent—bombard the individual and the person's hypersensitive antenna are picking up incorrect perceptions. In short, there is a breakdown in knowing the outside world correctly and accurately. (It is often said that addicts are people who hate having emotions yet have built-in hyperattentive emotional antennae. No wonder why they drink!) Too much emotional information flows in—not too little. The general results are two-fold. People can lash out at the world either as rageful or exceedingly moody or dramatic. Or, they may respond by retreating and becoming a doormat who is stepped on and over.

These responses feed into emotions and actions, and cause problems with impulse control. Depressed people do depressing things. Fearful people often do things or create reasons to make themselves more afraid. People who believe they are a fake (a common belief among addicts) go out of their way to prove they are not a fake and in so doing become bombastic, showy, arrogant, and know-it-alls. This results in more rejection and reinforcing feelings of phoniness because the showy behavior arouses suspicion and irritation in other people. People who feel the end is nigh act with wild abandon and show no care for the consequences of their behavior. They wreck their career and relational prospects by acting out in irresponsible ways, such as using alcohol or drugs excessively, and thereby reinforce their belief that the end is near. People who feel they are worthless do nothing to make themselves feel worthy and see alcohol or drugs as a way out of the hopeless morass. It is a self-constructed trap—tragic self-sabotage made all the more puzzling because the person often has no idea he is setting himself up for failure. Thus is the heartbreaking riddle of addiction.

When addicts receive faulty signals from the outside world, they respond emotionally in ways which they think are appropriate but which puzzle those around them. Indeed, others look on with astonishment or disgust. They ask, "How can this talented person throw away his life by behaving like that?" This is the perennial question of the alcoholic, for instance. How can someone so smart or handsome or talented or driven throw his life away? people ask. And it is all too often asked of the creative gay person who throws his career down the drain. Take Tennessee Williams and Truman Capote, for example, two brilliant playwrights whose lives spiraled down until both ultimately drank themselves to death in a "theater in the round" for all to see.

These skewed perceptions create desires that are out of sync with more normal adult behavior—behavior that aims for consideration, modesty, decent treatment of one's fellow man, rational negotiation toward worthwhile ends, and a general sense of "live and let live." These misperceptions instead create behaviors characterized by a lack of impulse control.

Their behaviors tend to begin in adolescence, the time at which many gay people begin to see themselves as different as well as the time that marks the beginning of alcohol and drug abuse for too many gay and bisexual people. The connection between many of these disorders and addiction is astounding. For instance, one study examining the connection between bipolar disorder and alcoholism concluded that more than 60 percent of people with bipolar disorder also have substance abuse problems. This world of co-occurring disorders is complex and fairly new. A person who has the disease of alcoholism as well as a co-occurring problem such as social anxiety, bipolar disorder, or antisocial disorder has a host of issues to contend with.

We will discuss the three clusters of co-occurring disorders in detail below, but Table 8.1 summarizes some general conclusions about co-occurring disorders in terms of general descriptions and among the three clusters.

THREE TYPES OF DISORDERS

There are three basic types of disorders and these three types of disorders can, I submit, be broken into general categories with respect to drug-taking as well as behavior types. This classification is, of course, a general type but can lead to some insight about the general types of behaviors and ways to help people caught in the vice of addiction *and* dysfunctional behavior that manifests itself in a lack of impulse control and relapse into drug-taking behaviors.

For the purposes of this chapter, then, we will look at the general behaviors of the various disorders, the dominant drug taking behavior among these people, and the general types of dysfunctional behaviors. In doing this, I have combined data from the *Diagnostic and Statistical Manual of Mental Disorders* with excellent work on co-occurring disorders from the Hazelden Foundation as well as the National Institute on Drug Abuse (NIDA) and the UCLA School of Family Medicine.

There is a need to demystify these names and create easy-to-understand classifications so that people can digest, discuss, and either embrace or discard what they learn. There is a need for a vulgate version of this bible of pathologies, which, like the Bible of the Middle Ages, is in a language that

Table 8.1. Statistics on Substance abuse and Co-occurring Disorders[1]

About one-third of people with ADHD have problems with substance abuse.
Heroin addicts have the fewest co-occurring disorders of all drug-users—about 25 percent.
Polydrug users have the highest prevalence of co-occurring disorders—nearly 60 percent.
On average, one in two substance abusers has a co-occurring disorder.
Alcohol-only substance abusers experience a disorder about 30 to 40 percent of the time.
About 60 percent of those with bipolar disorder have some form of alcohol or drug dependence.
People with substance abuse are about ten times more likely to have other mental health disorders.
Gay men are two to three times more likely to have substance abuse issues than heterosexuals.
Gay men have far higher rates of manic sexual behavior than heterosexuals.
Gay men are two times more likely to smoke than heterosexuals.

Prevalence-type	*Among Population*	*Among Substance Users*
Cluster A-loner	About 1.5%	15–20%
Cluster B-moody	1% in women; 3% in men	10–30% (Most common of addicts)
Cluster C-doormat	About 3%	Rarest; dependent most common in clinics

[1] Hazelden Foundation

no one understood and so it is inaccessible. (The Bible was parsed and argues to death, and so offered little nurturing or guidance about how to live. And it was feared rather than embraced, so many people used it to cook up absurd prescriptions for living. And the whole worship and study of it was often surrounded by fear rather than used to bring about better life.)

If we return to the warning of Kay Redfeld Jamison, we see that too many people want simple spiritual or psychological cures for addiction. And many others only seek medical cures for addiction. There is clearly room for both. What's more, there is a growing consensus that both are required. Outside of a few fringe groups on the West Coast of the United States, most Twelve Step groups accept and welcome input from medical professionals. And many psychologists, even begrudgingly, admit that spiritual solutions are appropriate. In recent times, both sides seem to be offering leeway. It is a given that you're going down a blind alley if you're just offering logotherapy/spiritual solutions or just offering medical solutions. The body, mind, and spirit are a triumvirate that can together overcome addiction.

In *The Sacred Cauldron: Psychotherapy as a Sacred Practice,* Lionel Corbett makes the point that, in the last few years, spirituality is being brought back into the therapist's office. He says, "For psychotherapy to ignore our spiritual instinct would be to ignore one of the main motivational factors within the personality." He quotes Abraham Maslow who refers to the process of "re-sacralization," the act of seeing the person as spiritual but also as genetic, behavioral, and psychological. His central point is that the whole dialogue of spirituality is couched in incorrect language of religion. Religion has nothing to do with it.[1] Spirituality, Corbett contends, is nothing more than a journey into how people deal with life's ultimate questions. It is natural that it should be part of the dialogue in the therapist's office.

In my book *Cravings for Deliverance*, I make the same point. I believe the entire foundation of the Twelve Step program comes from the agnostic and pragmatic thinking of William James and is absolutely non-religious. (In fact, there is a great deal of dismissive language toward religion in William James's seminal work *The Varieties of Religious Experience*.) James's influence on the Twelve Step movement was almost an animistic or humanistic one (definitely agnostic and deeply skeptical) where the act of self-surrender in the midst of a crisis of self-despair—all too often seen in the alcoholic's behavior—is an altogether human and profoundly common affair of the heart. It leads to the person falling back onto a higher power or a higher self just as his or her little self is falling to pieces. Again religion has nothing to do with it. In fact, James would go further and say that it is entirely private, barely known to the individual and precedes religion. Without spirituality, there simply is no religion. It comes much later, if at all.[2]

The purpose of this chapter is to laicize or offer some easily understood foundations for a topic that is certainly too complicated for an educated recovering addict or even many counselors. Then, we can connect the dots back to addiction and integrate some notions of spirituality into the solutions to these problems and arrive at a balanced view of psychological, medical, and spiritual health. In previous chapters, we attempted to see the diagnosis and prognosis of the gay or bisexual addict from the starting point of the drug: alcohol, cocaine, or CMA. In this chapter, we go in reverse order and look at the disorder (which may and often does precede the first drink or drug) and see what kinds of conclusions we can draw.

This book is already peppered with statistics which indicate that many alcoholics or addicts have co-occurring disorder, an addiction to a drug as well as some behavioral abnormality that is a heightened or odd deviation from otherwise normal behavior. For instance, we saw that two out of three people with bipolar disorder have some form of drug dependence, as do two out of three people with ADHD. The list goes on. It is my experience that while logotherapy and spiritual practices do go a long way toward healing, in addition to appropriate prescribed medications, it is impossible to maintain long-term sobriety without identifying, diagnosing, and offering medical treatment of these attending disorders, especially for gay men. If gay and bisexual men have rates of substance abuse three to four times higher than the heterosexual population, then we should assume that rates of co-occurring disorders are also elevated above those of the heterosexual population.

These statistics tell us that about 30 to 45 percent of people in treatment for addiction have some form of disorder that is beyond a substance-induced disorder. These numbers are far too high to ignore. It is becoming increasingly clear that the logotherapy/spiritual approach *and* medical/pharmacological approach must be merged and practitioners of both need to have an open mind.

Here are the three different groups of disorders on which many agree:

1. The distrustful or avoidant “loner” (this person is often one who abuses drugs)
2. The extremely moody “dramatist” (this person is often one who abuses alcohol)
3. The anxious and fearful “doormat” (this person is often one who is the spouse of an addict)

Of course, there is a high degree of subjectivity in diagnosing these disorders and my former mentors at UCLA (under whom I studied while completing an internship for a degree in drug and alcohol counseling) were also quick to warn about attaching such formal labels to people. The reasons are that:

a) There is a great deal of subjectivity about describing and diagnosing symptoms.
b) There is a profound difference between substance-induced disorders and more permanent conditions, which requires a good length of time before accurately naming a disorder.
c) People being diagnosed may themselves not be clear on their own past and may offer incorrect information or an inaccurate description of their situation.

THE DISTRUSTFUL OR AVOIDANT “LONER”

The first category is what we can, in general terms and for the sake of classification, call cluster A, or the “loner.” The table that follows describes behaviors not due to substance abuse and which have presented themselves for a considerable period of time. People in this category see the outside world as malevolent. Either they do not want relations because they see people as unworthy of trust or they want relations but do not trust anyone. These people are suspicious and aloof, and can be inflexible. They may have had these skewed perceptions since adolescence. Interestingly, these people will tend to abuse drugs over alcohol.

In recovery, such individuals may not want to be part of a group. They may not want to share with others and certainly would not want to work with a sponsor in a Twelve Step program. They may need the care of a psychiatrist and would benefit from a two-track recovery process where medications can be prescribed after a twenty- to thirty-day detoxification period. (This is because most people coming into a detox program most closely resemble the paranoid loner. Time is needed to allow the drugs to leave the system and for the person to gain a clearer picture of his past and identify patterns from adolescence related to particular kinds of behavior.)

Table 8.2. Cluster A: The "Odd and Alone" Drug Addict

Illness	*Thinking*	*Acting*	*Preferred Drug*	*Comment*
All Disorders	*not from drugs; skewed perception*	*no impulse control, begins in adolescence*	*NA*	*inflexible, pervasive; lifelong impairment*
Cluster A—NA?	**Avoidant, distrustful**	**Odd-Eccentric—"Loner" or "Weirdo"**		**wariness; relationships are depressing**
Paranoid	people are malevolent	no trust in anyone	cocaine, speed	persistent pattern of distrust
Schizoid	restricted emotions	does NOT want relations; prefers being alone	NA	no close relations at all
Schizotypal	terrified of rejection	wants relations, but too afraid	downers	suspicious, aloof, paranoid

THE EXTREMELY MOODY "DRAMATIST"

The second group is cluster B and can be described as the extremely moody victim or dramatist. In gay circles, this person may be described as a "drama queen." The drama queen needs validation since he has been wronged by the world and justifies outrageous behavior because of his (real or imagined) victimization. This behavior most often arises in an extremely sensitive person with low self-esteem and who may have an unstable sense of self. This very much reflects what was described in an earlier chapter of the closeted gay men as a divided self—a spy who is one thing to the straight world and another person inside. He dreads being caught in the lie of presenting himself as straight to his family, his community, and his church, as inside he has a hidden, dark side. This divided self cries out for integration and an indivisible self.

Table 8.3. The Alcoholic: A Moody and Angry Dramatist

Illness	*Thinking*	*Acting*	*Preferred Drug*	*Comment*
Cluster B—AA?	**extreme moods; victimization**	**Dramatic —Emotional —"Dramatist"**		
Histrionic	very low esteem	angry outbursts; demanding, suicidal	alcohol; benzos	vain and demanding and dependent
Narcissistic	I am entitled; easily hurt	arrogant, self-absorbed	polydrug	unstable personal life
Antisocial	lack of remorse; lying	reckless, irresponsible	polydrug*; most common	usually before 15; can be associated with schizophrenia, manic behavior; more common in males
Borderline	Unstable self-image, paranoid	no personal relationships	alcohol; benzos; broad detox	marked by impulsivity, frantic fear of abandonment; more common in females

*polydrug: alcohol, marijuana, heroin, cocaine, and meth

The process of finding one's integrated self often creates anguish and rage for a divided life and a lie that he too often believes comes from an intolerant society that engages in subtle and outright discrimination. Furthermore, gay men over forty-five remember the shabby treatment the gay community received by federal government policy makers during the height of the AIDS epidemic. Clearly, this would have aggravated the sense of victimization, as many gay men could justifiably conclude that the government turned away while tens of thousands of taxpaying citizens died from a public epidemic, an epidemic that was given improper attention from government policy, arguably based on discrimination.

While many of these disorders have attending substance use, which includes benzodiazepines, most of the categories include alcohol as the substance of choice. Alcohol quiets the voices and reduces the pain of past

HAZELDEN AND THE MATRIX MODEL OF UCLA: INCORPORATING CO-OCCURRING DISORDERS AND ADDICTION

The Matrix Model is designed as an outpatient model to help newly sober people gain a better grasp on the relationship between their thinking and emotions on the one hand and their behavior on the other. Classic cognitive-behavior therapy, it focuses first on making clear schedules for defined activity during the day to allow a person to steer himself or herself through the day. The idea is to let the person know where he or she is as the process of recovery unfolds. Measuring progress is also important.

Another vital element of Matrix is to be aware of triggers. It is important to identify them, prevent exposure to them, and deal with them in different ways. Attending Twelve Step meetings on a Friday night instead of going to happy hour is a simple example. The process is designed to short-circuit the process of trigger, thought, craving, use. The next part of this therapy involves developing thought-stopping techniques when cravings turn into obsessions. These techniques include visualizing a light switch that can be turned off, wearing a rubber band on the wrist and snapping it to remind oneself to say "No," or practicing breathing exercises. A fourth technique is to simply call someone.

Another important part of the process is about learning what to with common emotions such as anger, irritability, boredom, and loneliness. Much of this model resolves around creating structure, activities, and new relationships to fill time and create new meaning in one's life. Another aspect includes changing past behaviors such as stealing, lying, irresponsibility, and impulsive behavior, especially sexual behavior. Much of this focuses on the idea of HALT—that is, avoiding being hungry, angry, lonely, or tired.

Hazelden offers a similar model that is focuses on new developing relationships, new meaning, filled schedules. It is about getting a new mooring line and creating new relationships with people, thinking, and habits. Hazelden focuses more on how to integrate into the workforce as a sober person and on changing one's relationship to shame and guilt. Guilt is feeling bad about what we have done, whereas shame is feeling bad about who we are. Moving away from shame is vital to sobriety.

Exploring spirituality is an important element in the Hazelden approach. Motivation for recovery and staying truthful are both key notions to work on in the Hazelden model. In addition to pharmacological therapies, these two models of recovery are among the many that can be used to help overcome flawed thinking, shame-based behavior, and addictive thinking.

memories. It allows the gay man to deal with being overly dependent or having an unstable sexual life. It calms the manic behavior of the antisocial type who just never fit in. This may be especially true of the bisexual man who may feel that he fits into neither the gay camp nor the straight camp.

Again to reiterate the warnings of my UCLA mentor, all gay men exhibit some of these behaviors. We can be vain and we can cling too much. We may go through times when our personal lives are unstable. We may have frantic fear of abandonment. But it takes a period of sobriety—and some time with a qualified doctor—to determine whether we indeed have lifelong, profoundly disruptive behavior patterns that merit medication. Such behavior patterns are more than drug-induced mania or a reconditioning when it comes to dating and having stable relationships.

THE FEARFUL AND ANXIOUS "DOORMAT"

The third is cluster C and, in general, describes the fearful and anxious doormat who may not be able to defend himself or herself against the aggressive drunk or drug addict.

Table 8.4. The Fearful Doormat: The Codependent or Al-Anon Candidate

Illness	*Thinking*	*Acting*	*Preferred Drug*	*Comment*
Cluster C— (Al-Anon?)		**Anxious-Fearful— "Doormat"**		**need to be taken care of; clinging**
Avoidant	terrified of rejection	wants relations but afraid of them	alcohol, downers	avoid rejection at all costs
OCD	obsessed by rules, details	obsession w/ orderliness, control, perfection	NA	clear pattern and preoccupation for long periods
Dependent	excessive need for others	submissive; clinging; get abused	NA	tend to be in abusive relationships

These people may want order in their lives and may want to create order in others' lives. They have an obsession with rules and details, and may need to fix someone else in their own way. They may be the one who stays in a destructive relationship because it feels right. They do not want to be rejected, even if it is by an abusive addict. They would rather be in an abusive relationship than none at all. These men and women often find themselves in the rooms of Al-Anon, a program for people who are related to a person who abuses drugs or alcohol.

On this topic of the person who tends to have a disorder that causes dependence on a drug addict, there is a well-known treatment facility in London with a special session on "Family Day" that focuses on the spouses of drug and alcohol abusers. What does the counselor say about the person who stays with the addict when that addict continues bad behavior despite multiple warnings? He says point-blank and without any hesitation that the person who stays with the addict year after year and tolerates unbelievable behavior is just as sick as the addict. Cluster C may well describe this person.

The point here is that there may be real and legitimate reasons for the spouse to seek out professional help just as there is a need for the addict to seek help. A wise counselor once told me that alcoholics use the bottle to get drunk and escape their own problems. The abused spouses of alcoholics use the alcoholics as a bottle to escape their own problems. The alcoholic provides the spouse with a sense of danger, adventure, and the unknown. Over time, however, the behaviors become more tedious and outrageous. Spouses must face their own demons and this can be scary, so they might just decide to drown their sorrows in a merely metaphorical way and thereby escape their problems by losing themselves in the wild antics of the addict. Their low self-esteem just may be redeemed or raised if they can finally one day get the drunk to sober up.

In the context of gay life, there is a growing acceptance of gay couples who go about leading normal lives and who even have children in some countries. Nonetheless, we have a long way to go. In Asia, for instance, where most of the people on earth live, only one country has legalized gay marriage. It is Vietnam. Asia is still quite backward when it comes to offering any kind of acceptance or rights to gay men. Even in countries with liberal rights, a body of literature suggests that many gay couples deal with substance abuse and domestic violence. According to the Center for American Progress, 25 to 33 percent of same-sex relationships have had some form of domestic violence, significantly higher than in the heterosexual population. And physical and sexual abuse often co-occur.

For those who are closeted, one partner may threaten to "out" the other partner at work. Of course, one gay man may be more likely to fight back when assaulted by another gay man. And police may not report such incidents because they feel that two gay men can "work things out." Also, many gay men who perceive that gay relationships are demonized or seen as cursed by the heterosexual community are reluctant to say anything about what is happening for fear that society may further identify same-sex relationships as inherently dysfunctional.[3] In sum, gay men who are partners with an addict may qualify for some diagnosis in cluster C, but only a qualified doctor in counseling should make this call.

In the "other" category, we see the general topic of bipolar disorder, PTSD, ADHD, and GAD among others. Although we lay out this category for the purposes of unity and completion, these are way beyond the scope of this book. It's sufficient here to note that we have gone into great detail about PTSD in previous chapters. We showed that there is ample literature on the topic to indicate that PTSD is a wide-scale phenomenon in the gay community and is often undiagnosed. As with the many thousands of military "wounded warriors" who may have PTSD, it is given short shrift in the gay community because many think it is over-diagnosed. Simply put, many find it impossible to swallow the reality that tens of thousands of gay men may have PTSD just as they are unable to accept that there are tens of thousands of soldiers returning from battle who have this disorder. The numbers are so large as to beggar the imagination. But there we have it.

Table 8.5.

Illness	*Thinking*	*Acting*	*Preferred Drug*	*Comment*
Other				
Depressive	death; worthlessness	no pleasure in any activity; weight loss	polydrug; often drug induced	usually 2 weeks; hypersomnia, indecisive, thoughts of death
Manic	grandiosity; flighty	talkative; hyper-focus; sex/buying sprees	polydrug; often drug induced	insomnia; interest in pleasure activity where pain comes afterward—buying, sex sprees
Generalized Anxiety	worry; irritable; keyed up; anxious	restless, tired, insomnia	responds to group well	ongoing w/out drugs
Schizophrenia	hallucination, delusion	disorganized speech, behavior; no affect	garbage can drug use	6 mths to 1 year; considered psychotic
ADHD	no attention, listening;	avoids tasks, activities; squirms; blurts out	35% of ADHD use drugs	begins in high school; high relapse rate
PTSD	nightmares, amnesia, detached	change in life behavior; outbursts; insomnia	opiates, cocaine	event comes from actual or threatened death

DUAL DIAGNOSIS REQUIRES DUAL RECOVERY: RECOGNITION OF POWERLESSNESS OVER ALCOHOL AND BIPOLAR DISORDER

Henry, a forty-nine-year-old man American from New York, was a highly successful businessman who had received undergraduate and graduate degrees from Ivy League universities. By the age of forty, he began having difficulty keeping his personal and professional life together and experienced greater mood swings, long periods of isolation, and high-strung erratic behavior. He would watch the news cycle on CNN over and over again, drinking one bottle of white wine after the other. He noticed at other times that his mind would become "speedy" and he imagined there were many conversations going on at the same time. He felt as if he were crazy. He referred to the inside of his head a nonstop committee of endless debate that was fruitless and disturbing. The first drink made all that go away, but the consequences from drinking were catastrophic. In one year, he woke up in three different hospitals with an IV drip in his arm and no idea of how he got there.

His life took a turn for the worse and he could no longer focus on work. His increasingly high-strung and sometimes bizarre behavior was alienating his family. His emotions became more extreme and his drinking became out of control as he tried to quiet his mind and keep himself from falling apart. Eventually, he reached the point where he just did not care if he woke up the next day.

Henry tried to get sober through AA meetings, but did not seem to get it. Though he was in and out of the rooms for a few years, he still found himself completely disillusioned with life and lost his will to live. His occasional highs were higher and his lows were lower and growing dangerously close together. He went to at least eight rehabs and nothing helped. Henry was a speeding car with no brakes to stop the Indy 500 race going around endlessly in his head— except alcohol.

He finally happened upon a psychiatrist who listened carefully to Henry's story. It was clear to this psychiatrist that Henry had suffered from bipolar disorder his whole adult life and was a time bomb ready to go off. He told Henry that continuous sobriety would be difficult if he did not get his bipolar disorder under control through medication and therapy.

Henry knew that drinking was not the solution, but he needed *something* to make his mind shut up. In Twelve Step parlance, he did not want to surrender to a chemical power greater than himself. Within AA he found a constructive, caring, but, he thought, slightly misplaced message that people should not let medication take the place of social, spiritual, and personal recovery. He sometimes noticed people's eyes rolling when he would discuss his bipolar diagnosis in meetings. He knew the people in AA had good intentions, but they were unwittingly discouraging him from following a life-saving regimen of medication *and* also participating in a program of recovery in AA.

Were his previous efforts at getting sober through AA alone completely futile? In the end, Henry did not want to interpret it this way. Rather, he saw that he simply was never given a correct diagnosis. He suffered from alcoholism *and* bipolar disorder, something he now sees as crystal clear in hindsight. Today, he is an active and happy member of AA and also sees himself as a member in another Twelve Step program of sorts where he knows he is powerless over his bipolar disorder and needs to listen to and follow the instructions of his doctor. His life is unmanageable without medication and therapy. His program of dual recovery from a dual diagnosis offers him an invaluable camaraderie of fellow travelers, and his medications offer him a calmness of mind and greater ease to process life. This offers him detachment to respond to life in a more measured and mature way, which endears him to colleagues. Today, he is a leader in a cutting-edge technology firm and is happier than ever.

The treatment on this topic in *The Velvet Rage* is excellent. And it certainly matches my own experience of working with gay men in recovery who, years into recovery, describe symptoms that resemble PTSD. Many gay men do not want to admit they have it because they think it is almost an insult to soldiers who have "earned it" through battle. But so many gay men over age forty-five have lost many friends and lovers to HIV-related illness. One heartbreaking story is from someone I knew in Los Angeles who got sober in 1985. He said by 1990, every one of the people he got sober with in the rooms of AA was dead from AIDS. His whole "home group" in Santa Monica was wiped out from the disease.

Gay men in their twenties live with the threat of contracting HIV or are living with it. Many have concluded that should just "contract HIV" and get it over with rather than living with the chronic anxiety that they will become infected with this potentially life-threatening illness during the act of sex with another man. Many men who live with HIV now do so with a degree of calm and acceptance, but there is an undeniable lingering stigma attached to it, especially in many urban areas in Asia. Some brave men are leaders in gaining rights for those with HIV and are happy and well adjusted in their approach to daily health and regimens. However, many live with the fear of getting it or with the financial, emotional, and social anxiety of living with it day to day. This absolutely takes its toll on the community and is a drag on mental health, since it leads to anxiety, depression, and a chronic fear of the unknown.

NOTES

1. Corbett, Lionel, *The Sacred Cauldron: Psychotherapy as a Spiritual Practice*. Chiron Publications. 2011.

2. Schulte, Paul, *Cravings for Deliverance*, Lantern Press, New York. 2014.

3. Fact Sheet on Domestic Violence in the LGBT Community, Center for American progress June 11, 2011.

Chapter Nine

Reflections

A Failure of Imagination in Helping the Gay Community?

Gay men in the United States still face many obstacles that heterosexuals are not aware of. As mentioned in this book, the alarming realities become clear if we out the starkest ones in all their ugliness:

1. It is legal in twenty-nine states for gay and transgender people to be denied employment, fired, or discriminated against because of their sexual orientation.
2. Forty-three percent of gay men have experienced discrimination in the workplace.
3. Fifty-six percent of gay men report some form of discrimination in housing based on their orientation.
4. Gay men are two times more likely not to have health care than heterosexual men.
5. Almost half of runaways in the United States are gay, bisexual, or lesbian.
6. Gay men have addiction rates that are three to four times higher than the general population.
7. Suicide attempts for gay, bisexual, or lesbian people are between two and three times higher than the general population.
8. Being gay is a felony in more than seventy five countries and it is a capital offense (death penalty) in at least eleven countries.
9. Rates of HIV infection for gay men continue to climb in all major cities and CMA addiction rates are also climbing. Intravenous use of CMA in the gay community is out of control in many urban areas.
10. Most important, however, is that gay and lesbian Twelve Step meetings are proliferating everywhere. Rehabs for gays, bisexuals, and lesbians are springing up all over the world. There is hope and we are all designed to heal whether we are gay, straight, bisexual, or lesbian.

So, if the gay community were a person, what should we do with a seemingly wayward individual who very definitely shows deterioration in terms of drug and alcohol abuse as well as unsafe sexual practices that lead to very expensive treatments and unknown long-term medical consequences? If we return to the analogy of left-handedness, the gay person often knows in early adolescence that he is different. Like a left-handed person who constantly needs to adjust to a right-handed world, the gay person feels dislocated in a heterosexual world. He feels out of place and lacks a lifelong point of reference of belonging. There is a constant need to "fit in" with a world that is foreign in many ways. It is a constant discomfort.

The result of lifelong anxiety of not "belonging" or not being explicitly invited into society (and in many societies explicitly being asked to leave) is a sense of being plain lost without a point of reference. If a person is even slightly inclined to drug and alcohol addiction, this feeling of being on the outside (in addition to having secrets and shame) is like a pilot light under a water heater waiting to be unleashed. No wonder the gay and bisexual community has addiction rates that are three to four times higher than the rest of the population. If the general population has an a substance abuse rate of about 10 percent, this means the rate of substance abuse for gay and bisexual men could be as high as 30 percent. Indeed, the "chemsex study" from London that was highlighted in earlier chapters shows that the addiction rate for the gay community is *at least* 30 percent and the HIV transmission rate is between 14 and 19 percent. And these cases continue to rise, as does the incidence of slamming crystal meth.

TAKING ACTION

Some literature suggests that we need to take a compassionate, nonjudgmental, and gentle approach to this problem in order not to offend anyone. The chemsex study recommended distributing pamphlets that suggest, in a nonjudgmental manner, how gay men can use drugs in ways that are less harmful to them. I have to admit that, after reading an excellent report documenting an appalling level of substance abuse with dangerous combinations of drugs, widespread slamming of crystal meth, and high levels of HIV transmission, I was surprised by the tepid recommendations. This report comes from a presumably heterosexually dominated institution like the revered School of Hygiene and Tropical Medicine. Do the authors feel that recommending more severe measures (which are appropriate in the midst of any epidemic?) to the gay community smacks of finger-wagging or condescension? The level of politically correct language found throughout medical journals (more than one hundred were quoted in this book) borders on the absolutely Victorian. No one wants to say that there is a seemingly out-of-control spread of HIV through unsafe sex, which is mostly a function of the abuse of CMA (increasingly slammed) and which then invites a cascading abuse of other drugs.

The question we have to answer is whether treating the gay and bisexual community this way is tantamount to a codependent wife who occasionally offers stern but inconsequential warnings to her husband who drives while drunk and beats his children. Wouldn't we want to offer sage advice to the wife and tell her to detach with love? Wouldn't we want to suggest that she should use tough love? Most important, wouldn't we want to tell the wife that she is doing great harm to her husband in the long run by allowing him to escape the consequences of his actions with alcohol or drug abuse? Wouldn't we end up recommending that the wife take harsh and definitive action—that she leave her husband and take the children—in order to bring him to his senses? Should we be asking the same questions of the medical community that refuses to act in tough love and which consistently allows people in the gay community to seemingly escape the consequences of their actions?

These are the thorny questions we must ask. This is most definitely *not* a matter of whether to be politically correct or not. It is a question of whether the community of researchers and clinicians wants to accept that its desire to avoid controversy is tantamount to the codependent wife giving the car keys to her drunk husband with a gentle warning not to hurt anyone. It is a question of whether the community of doctors and clinicians has a dysfunctional or codependent relationship with the gay community and refuses to take a stand on controversial issues.

On a related issue, in an earlier chapter I cited a fascinating study that looked at depression, childhood abuse, substance abuse, and spousal abuse and their relationship or influence on HIV transmission. The intriguing conclusion (which matches my own experience in working with gay men in recovery) is that a cascading effect of all of the four dynamics *together* often dominates the scene and creates a locomotive of powerful self-destructive behaviors. Indeed, such behaviors have their own momentum that make it hard for many gay and bisexual men to stop having unsafe sex, especially when they are high or intoxicated. This is even true for many gay men who have long-term sobriety. After so many years of abuse, discrimination, stigmatization, low-grade trauma, or just seeing others get sick or die from HIV-related illnesses, they have a sense of "Who Cares? The future makes no difference." The way I see it, many men with this attitude have taken up danger-seeking or reckless behavior which, as I pointed out in the middle of the book, speaks to widespread PTSD within the gay community.

If this is the case, and I am certain it is, then countering it requires a multidisciplinary and coordinated effort. Clinicians with very specific expertise need to allow themselves to become uncomfortable. Psychiatrists need to engage the counselor. The counselor needs to engage the Twelve Step expert. The Twelve Step expert needs to engage the psychologist. And the psychologist needs to engage the rabbi. The study by the CDC confirms this. In other words, helping the gay and bisexual community by treating the problem as an epidemic falls short. Treating the problem as an issue of drug dependence falls short. Seeing the problem through the lens of a psychiatrist is not enough. And seeing it from the view of a traumatized individual helps but does not go far enough either. We need a more aggressive and uncomfortable embracing of one discipline with another. And each of these branches must ask if tepid language, which is intended to be politically correct, is actually a disguise for codependent language that lets the community off the hook, that allows a set of behaviors to continue even though there is a solution.

While writing this book and exploring the various angles of treating addiction, I have concluded that the best approach for treating those in the gay community includes viewing the group as one where too many are suffering from moderate to severe PTSD. (Too many of the symptoms of too many gay and bisexual men add up to PTSD!) This book has offered many options, treatments, and programs for these men, some of which have been adapted from approaches used to treat the community of veterans who are also overwhelmed by their own "wounded warriors." (In this book, we have called these gay and bisexual men "rainbow warriors.")

It is true that veterans themselves are taking matters into their own hands to help fellow veterans. (One of these is a very admirable organization in Australia called www.soldieron.org.au that supports and creates programs to help veterans get jobs, readjust to life given health issues, participate in social activities, raise money for psychical and mental therapeutic programs, create donations to worthy charities, and construct centers where men can spend time and heal. This is an ideal of what the gay community could also do to create centers for younger gay men to rest, heal, recover from addiction, and look for job opportunities.)

Many gay men are happy, well adjusted, and stable and have loving partners. This book is most definitely not for them. But too many gay and bisexual men are desperately looking for direction, help, and advice on life issues. And a very large proportion of them are dealing with substance abuse and issues of domestic abuse, sexual compulsion, and risky sexual activity with strangers, and they need help with professional direction and personal relationships. In this context, a multidisciplinary approach that can offer more assertive guidance for gay and bisexual men seems entirely appropriate if it is done in a respectful way. I am suggesting an end to milquetoast recommendations that border on cliché and are tantamount to the codependent wife who laments her husband's drunk driving but says nothing about it. Many wise counselors I know think that the behavior of the codependent wife is as sick as the behavior of the alcoholic who drives drunk. Clinicians, psychiatrists, and doctors need to detach with love and treat gay and bisexual men as adults who need and deserve the full and unvarnished truth. And these gay and bisexual men need respectful but firm advice not how to kill themselves in safer ways but how to create an ideal of living a fuller and richer life without drugs and alcohol.

On a related topic, the medical community needs to stop playing down the longer term effects of CMA use. Gay men are not stupid—they can read articles from scientific journals on the Internet. If anything, the noise level on the destructive effects should be ratcheted up. Gay men who abuse CMA come to Twelve Step meetings and it is said that their experience is a revolving door. There needs to be a more vocal message that if a gay or bisexual man wants to heal from CMA abuse, he needs more than a Twelve Step meeting schedule or outpatient facility. He needs a long-term facility. The best doctors in this field have come to this conclusion. If the medical community is serious about treating these men, more money and facilities will be needed. Without these facilities, I fear we are all just spinning our wheels.

On the issue of relapse prevention, it seems that those most at risk are Latino and African American men who are in their early twenties and who have a few years of college. Far more aggressive language on the dangers of CMA is needed. There may be a hue and cry from some on this, but if the warnings can help even a few avoid the devastating consequences of CMA abuse, then so be it. Clubs, churches, community centers, junior colleges, and local jails should all have explicit advertisements in bathrooms, on bar napkins, in hallways, and in cafeterias warning about CMA. After all, so many studies highlight CMA as the gateway drug to HIV as well as to other accompanying drugs like GHB, cocaine, mephedrone, and ecstasy.

Another related issue is ideals or goals. In any attempt to get a person or an organization to change behavior, the creation of goals and ideals is paramount. Where does a person or an organization wish to be in six or twelve months? What kinds of behaviors and regimen are required to achieve these goals? What short-term goals are achievable versus long-term goals? In the case of the gay community, there is too much emphasis on slowing the rate of change of HIV. There is too much emphasis on being politically correct when it comes to reducing CMA use. We are seeing nothing but continued rises in HIV and continued rises in slamming of CMA. The obvious question that arises is why is there not a concerted effort to organize medical, psychiatric, counseling, police, and public policy players to create more dramatic goals or ideals. For instance, what kind of behavior change or policy implementation would cause a 50 percent drop in HIV transmission? What kinds of policy tools or changes in the medical, police, counseling, or psychiatric approach within the gay community would bring about a 50 percent drop in CMA use? Why can't we aim for more aggressive and more startling ideals and goals? Right now, the gay community is creaking under its own weight when it comes to professional, social, emotional, and medical costs to HIV transmission and CMA abuse.

One option that is often discussed but which is controversial is contingency management. Drs. Shoptaw, Larkins, and Reback at UCLA and Friends Research Institute frequently mention the idea of contingency management in treating CMA. The cost-benefit analysis of these programs often makes them seem worthwhile even though many gripe that we should not pay people to stay sober. Yet, much work has been done on this and the results do appear to pay off. Of course, men with a history of drug abuse who "pee clean" in random drug tests are not given cash. Instead, they are given vouchers for groceries and other necessities. Again, there is controversy here, but the longer term benefits often outweigh the costs.[1]

LOUD AND CLEAR

In conclusion, we need to have more overt and louder discussions about the kind of language that can be used to describe the profound crisis of drug addiction and HIV prevalence in the gay community. Cities like Hong Kong and Singapore in the early stages of CMA and HIV prevalence need guidance in how to stamp out problems that can cost billions of dollars and untold personal, health, and professional damage to people's lives. For instance, my anecdotal evidence is that CMA slamming in Hong Kong and Singapore is just getting under way and little if anything is being done. Goals and ideals for HIV and CMA reduction need to be articulated, even though they may be unachievable in the short term but which are possible in the longer term.

Twelve Step programs are fairly new in China but are proliferating at a terrific pace, mostly through Skype and other social media. The problem of CMA in China is becoming problematic only in the past few years. For instance, in December 2013, the Chinese police had to bring in paramilitary troops to smash a well-organized and well-defended CMA ring in Guangdong province, a large province of 70 million people adjacent to Hong Kong. The police found three tonnes of finished CMA and twenty-three tonnes of raw material chemicals for the production of CMA. This should serve as a wakeup call to policy makers in Southeast Asia about the prevalence of CMA. Authorities in Hong Kong and Singapore impose very tough sentences in excess of fifteen years in prison for trafficking drugs like CMA. At the same time, the facilities to aid gay men who are addicted to CMA scarcely exist. This must change.

LAYING OUT THE ISSUES OF LONG-TERM DAMAGE FROM CMA

Most gay men are intelligent and have access to the Internet, meaning they are fully capable of being informed of potential consequences of drug use. I have had many conversations with gay men who have used crystal meth, and many say that they read of dire consequences about its use but then their doctors downplayed the consequences. This leaves them to conclude that it must be okay to use and they can safely ignore the dangerous warnings laid out in other literature. This is another example where psychiatrists and therapists need to stop treating gay men like children and start treating them like adults. This means equipping them with all of the generally accepted information about the long-term effects of CMA. These include depression, heart arrhythmia, strokes, cardiomyopathy, congestive heart failure, and moderate brain damage that prevents the person from having more normal emotional responses to things like success, happy events, or successful relationships. One publication (*Journal of American Psychiatry*) spelled it out loud and clear, and professionals in the drug addiction community owe it to adult gay men to tell them about the drug's consequences in unequivocal ways:

The study concluded that methamphetamine abuse could cause "long-lasting changes in dopamine cell activity and persistence of amotivation as well as anhedonia (depression) in detoxified methamphetamine abusers. While the brain's power to heal itself always surprises us, and while protracted abstinence of CMA can reverse some of the methamphetamine-induced alterations in brain function, other deficits can persist for a long period of time.[1] . . . Other side effects include stomach cramps, shaking, tooth loss, anxiety, insomnia, paranoia, and hallucinations; these are in addition to the structural changes to the brain discussed above."

Note

1. Gene-Jack Wang, M.D.; Nora D. Volkow, M.D.; Linda Chang, M.D.; Eric Miller, Ph.D.; et al, Partial Recovery of Brain Metabolism in Methamphetamine Abusers After Protracted Abstinence. *American Journal of Psychiatry* 2004; 161:242–248.

Asian capitals will need assistance from cities like Los Angeles, New York, San Francisco, and London when it comes to dealing with drugs like CMA and the spread of HIV in the gay population. In Hong Kong alone, there are about 5,000 cases of HIV from virtually none eight or ten years ago. The Twelve Step program in Hong Kong has established the first ever Crystal Methamphetamine Anonymous meeting in Asia. More will surely follow.

Another anecdotal data point is that one of the few rehabs in Southeast Asia located in Thailand recently treated a group of addicts of which one in four were crystal meth addicts. The problem is proliferating, and this book may help policy makers in Asian cities as well as those in the West.

ASIA IS LEARNING QUICKLY BUT NEEDS HELP WITH A GAY COMMUNITY AT SEA

Asia is slowly adapting the language of the West when it comes to identifying mental disorders in the gay community. It is now asking questions about why people in the gay community have high rates of substance abuse, poor life outcomes, and high rates of anxiety and depression. One study explored a large group of gay and bisexual Japanese men and churned up some startling data. Of the 1,025 respondents who identified as gay or bisexual:

- 15 percent of the men reported a history of attempted suicide
- 70 percent showed high levels of anxiety
- 13 percent showed high levels of depression
- 83 percent reported experiencing school bullying
- 60 percent were verbally harassed for being perceived as homosexual

This study concluded that suicidality was connected with verbal abuse, disclosure of sexual identity, anonymous sexual hookups, and not having a university degree. In other words, these gay men in Japan were struggling with trauma, rejection, isolation, and a lack of focus in life, which leads to poor outcomes. Presumably, this group would likely have high levels of alcohol and drug abuse but the study did not explore this angle.[1] It is not just Hong Kong and Singapore that are dealing with skyrocketing levels of drug and alcohol abuse in the gay community. China, Japan, Korea, and India also are slowly but necessarily bringing into the open the issue of gay and bisexual culture and helping these individuals integrate into society. There is a long way to go and as research continues, I would not be the least bit surprised if levels of alcohol and drug abuse in the gay community in these countries are as high or higher than in the West.

Note

1. Y Hidaka, D Operario, Attempted suicide, psychological health and exposure to harassment among Japanese homosexual, bisexual or other men questioning their sexual orientation recruited via the internet. *J Epidemiol Community Health* 2006;60:962–967.

Compassion and unconditional positive regard must come first for any person who is seeking treatment for drug addiction. But there is also the thorny issue of the Hippocratic Oath, which says, "Do no harm." Watering down and allowing people to escape the consequences of their own behavior can, indeed, do great harm. At the rate things are going, highly concentrated gay boroughs and towns like Lambeth, Chelsey, San Francisco, West Hollywood, and Rio de Janeiro could end up with HIV infection rates in excess of 25 percent and rates of CMA slamming of 50 percent. Some people think that the dispensing of advice is a matter of whether language is or is not politically correct. I believe that the use of language by the medical, psychological, and psychiatric community which is overly correct or which is drained of power and authority is tantamount to engaging in a highly codependent and self-destructive relationship with the gay community. Overly correct messages essentially tell the gay community to go ahead and drive drunk with a mere tap on the wrist.

The appalling statistics, especially those of the London Chemsex study, speaks to a community which needs a call to arms to intervene and offer a way out by strong leadership. In fact, the vast majority of excellent scientific studies about gay men and drugs end up with similar conclusions which are a bland diet of polite finger-wagging, benevolent reflection about future implications of HIV transmission or a call for more government brochures for the public on the consequences of substance abuse. Many of these journals do not even want to use the world drug addiction. This is not good enough when there is a serious health crisis which is growing more serious by the year.

There is a need for imagination and bold action. There is a need for goals and ideals of where the community could be in one or three years. One of the conclusions of the London Chemsex report is that only one third of the men thought they had a substance abuse problem. Two thirds say they did not. Indeed, addiction is considered by many to be a 'disease of denial.' Many addicts will often say they do not have a problem even when they are out of work, sick and under legal indictment. We should expect people in the midst of their disease of addiction to express denial and constantly engage in relapse. This is, in fact, the nature of the disease of addiction: denial and relapse. To take the advice of the patient in this regard makes no sense at all.

The health crisis which is playing out in many Western cities is only in the early stages in Asian cities. The characteristics of this full blown health crisis in the West—and which is at a nascent stage in cities like Hong Kong, Singapore, Jakarta, Seoul and Taipei are: 1) highly expensive HIV medications for a significant minority of the gay population; 2) deaths from overdose and drug-induced suicide; 3) chronic unemployment for younger gay and bisexual men (as well as for older professionals who get caught in the trap of CMA) who cannot hold down jobs given the negative consequences of drug use;

4) public officials who give up on the gay community because they see a lack of "self-control" given 'out of control' drug abuse; 5) a drug and alcohol treatment infrastructure which breaks under the weight of numbers; 6) an absence of political leadership given earlier than usual death of the 'elders' from drug and alcohol abuse as well as long-term health consequences from HIV; 7) growing social isolation of individuals from the side effects of drug abuse; and 8) an unwillingness on the part of the entire community to take a brutally honest look at the connection between mental disorders and drug addiction. Herein lies the problem. How do we find the right language to initiate a frank and candid discussion on these vital but thorny issues? The data points indisputably toward an accelerating devolution of the overall physical and mental health of a significant minority of the gay community. Is it time for the gay community to take off the gloves?

Asian cities look to those in the West with experience in this epidemic. Is it high time to set an example for cities that have not been decimated by HIV and CMA, and offer them meaningful language, tough tactics, viable strategies as well as long-term goals and ideals to prevent yet another set of public health catastrophes across the Pacific Rim? I say, yes, the time has come to change the language, the goals, the ideals, and the strategies. What has been tried so far has been a failure of imagination.

NOTE

1. Ling Murtaugh K, Krishnamurti T, Reback CJ, Shoptaw, S, Spend today, clean tomorrow: predicting methamphetamine abstinence in a randomized controlled trial, *Health Psychology*, 2013, Sept (958–66).

Appendix

Death Study for Gay Men Who Went Through Treatment

HIV Negative (Neg N=33)	*DEAD* (Dead N=9)	*HIV Positive* (Poz N=67)	
1st drink	13 yrs	17 yrs	18 yrs
1st meth use	23 yrs	27 yrs	29 yrs
R U Addicted?(yes)	100%	89%	82%
Felony (yes)	44%	5%	9%
Antidepressants (yes)	66%	88%	60%
Bipolar	55%	6%	3%
Smoker (yes)	80%	31%	18%
IV User	55%	40%	15%
Sex (always/often)	n/a	87%	88%
Sex-compulsive-yes	77%	79%	82%
Hepatitis	77%	37%	27%
Family alcoholism	75%	77%	82%

Death Study results: continued

	DEAD	*HIV Positive*	*HIV Negative*
Diabetes	33%	33%	45%
School/college	12th grade	1.3 yrs	2.5 yrs
Unsafe sex	100%	100%	66%
HIV Age	26	29	n/a
Years w/ HIV	15	9	n/a
Death Age (mean)	41 (2002)	n/a	n/a
Year born	1963	1962	1962
1st Drink to meth (yrs)	10	10	10

Bibliography

American Psychiatric Association. *Diagnostic and Statistical Manual of Mental Disorders.* 4th edition. Arlington, VA: American Psychiatric Publishing, 2013.

Beitchman, Joseph H., et al. "A Review of the Long-Term Effects of Child Sexual Abuse." *Child Abuse and Neglect* 16, no. 1 (1992): 101–18.

Bentley, Jack. "A Short History of PTSD: From Thermophlae to Hue: Soldiers Have Always Had a Disturbing Reaction to War." *The Veteran*, 1991.

Berg, R. C., and M. W. Ross. "The Second Closet: A Qualitative Study of HIV Stigma among Seropositive Gay Men in a Southern U.S. City." *International Journal of Sexual Health*, 26, no. 3. October 2013.

Bloor, M., N. McKeganey, and M. Bernard. "An Ethnographic Study of HIV-Related Risk Practices among Glasgow Rent Boys and Their Clients: Report of a Pilot Study." *AIDS Care: Psychological and Socio-medical Aspects of AIDS/HIV* 2, no. 1 (September 2007): 17–24.

Bolen, Rebecca M., and Maria Scannapieco. "Prevalence of Child Sexual Abuse: A Corrective Meta-analysis." *Social Service Review* 73, no. 3 (1999): 281.

Bourne, A, Reid D, Hickson F, Torres Rueda S, Weatherburn P. *The ChemsexSstudy: Drug Use in Sexual Settings among Gay & Bisexual Men in Lambeth, Southwark & Lewisham.* London: Sigma Research, London School of Hygiene & Tropical Medicine, 2014.

Boyd, C. J., S. E. McCabe, and H. d'Arcy. "Ecstasy Use among College Undergraduates: Gender, Race and Sexual Identity." *Journal of Substance Abuse Treatment* 24, no. 3 (April 2003): 209–15.

Brahmam, Ginnela, Kodavalla, et al. "Sexual Practices, HIV and Sexually Transmitted." n.d.

Brahmam, G., V. Kodavella, H. Rajkumar, H. K. Rachakulla, S. Kallam, S. P. Myakala, R. S. Paranjape, M. D. Gupte, L. Ramakrishnan, A. Kohli, and B. M. Ramesh. "Sexual Practices, HIV and Sexually Transmitted Infections among Self-identified Men Who Have Sex with Men in Four High HIV Prevalence States in India." *AIDS* 22 (December 2008): 45–57.

Briere, John, and Diana M. Elliott. "Prevalence and Psychological Sequelae of Self-Reported Childhood Physical and Sexual Abuse in a General Population Sample of Men and Women." *Child Abuse and Neglect* 27, no. 10 (October 2003): 1205–22.

Buxton, A. P. "Writing Our Own Script: How Bisexual Men and Their Heterosexual Wives Maintain Their Marriages After Disclosure." *Journal of Bisexuality* 1, no. 2–3 (October 2008): 155–89.

Cáceres, C., K. Konda, M. Pecheny, A. Chatterjee, and R. Lyerla. "Estimating the Number of Men Who Have Sex with Men in Low and Middle Income Countries." 2006.

Carrier, M. "Mexican Male Sexuality." *Journal of Homosexuality* 11, no. 1–2 (1985): 75–86.

Cohen, M. *Coming Out to My Wife.* February 15, 2013.

Coleman, E. "Bisexual and Gay Men in Heterosexual Marriage: Conflicts and Resolutions in Therapy." *Journal of Homosexuality* 7, nos. 2–3 (1982): 93–103.

Corbett, Lionel. *The Sacred Cauldron: Psychotherapy as a Spiritual Practice.* Wilmette, IL: Chiron Publications, 2011.

Crawford, David. *Easing the Ache: Gay Men Recovering from Compulsive Behaviors.* New York: Penguin Group, 1990.

Daley, Dennis. *Coping with Dual Disorders: Addiction and Psychiatric Illness.* Hazelden Foundation, 2003.

Denizet-Lewis, Benoit. "The Scientific Quest to Prove Bisexuality Exists." *New York Times*, March 20, 2014.

Downes, Alan. *The Velvet Rage: Overcoming the Pain of Growing Up Gay in a Straight Man's World.* 2nd edition . New York: Da Capo, 2012.

Fact Sheet on Domestic Violence in the LGBT Community. Center for American Progress, 2011.

Findling, R. L., B. L. Gracious, N. K. McNamara, E. A. Youngstrom, C. A. Demeter, L. A. Branicky, and J. R. Calabrese. "Rapid, Continuous Cycling and Psychiatric Co-Morbidity in Pediatric Bipolar I Disorder." *Bipolar Disorders* 3, no. 4 (August 2014): 202–10.

Finkelhor, David. "The Prevention of Childhood Sexual Abuse." *The Future of Children* 19, no. 2 (2009): 169–94.

Frankl, Viktor. *Man's Search for Meaning.* Beacon Press, 1956.

Fraser, Andrew. "On Trial for Being Gay." *Attitude*, June 2014.

Grossman, Arnold. "Growing Up with a 'Spoiled Identity': Lesbian, Gay and Bisexual Youth at Risk." *Journal of Gay and Lesbian Social Services* 6, no. 3 (1997): 45–56.

Hatzenbuehler, Mark L. "The Social Environment and Suicide Attempts in Lesbian, Gay, and Bisexual Youth." *Pediatrics*, April 2011.

Hatzenbuehler, Mark L., Katie A. McLaughlin, Katherine M. Keyes, and Deborah S. Hasin. "The Impact of Institutional Discrimination on Psychiatric Disorders in Lesbian, Gay, and Bisexual Populations: A Prospective Study." *AJPH*, March 2010: 452–459.

Hershberger, S. L., N. W. Pilkington, and A. R. D' Augelli. "Predictors of Suicide Attempts among Gay, Lesbian, and Bisexual Youth." *Journal of Adolescent Research* 12, no. 4 (October 1997): 477–97.

Hidaka, Y., D Operario. "Attempted Suicide, Psychological Health and Exposure to Harassment among Japanese Homosexual, Bisexual or Other Men Questioning Their Sexual Orientation Recruited via the Internet." *J Epidemiol Community Health* 60 (2006): 962–7.

Holmes, William C., and Gail B. Slap. "Sexual Abuse of Boys: Definition, Prevalence, Correlates, Sequelae, and Management." *Journal of the American Medical Association* 280, no. 21 (1998): 1855–62.

Jeffriesa, W. L., B. Dodgeb, and T. G. M. Sandfort. "Religion and Spirituality among Bisexual Black Men in the USA." *Culture, Health & Sexuality: An International Journal for Research, Intervention and Care* 10, no. 5 (2008): 463–47.

James, W. *Varieties of Religious Experience.* New York: Barnes & Noble Classics, 2004.

Jamison, Kay Redfield. "To Know Suicide." *New York Times*, August 20, 2014.

Jenny, Carole, Thomas A. Roesler, and Kimberly L. Poyer. "Are Children at Risk for Sexual Abuse by Homosexuals?" *Pediatrics* 94, no. 1 (July 1994): 41–44.

Jourard, Sidney. "Sidney Jourard Lecture." Florida Presbyterian College, September 27, 1969.

King, M., J. Semlyen, S. S. Tai, H. Killaspy, D. Osborn, and D. Popelyk. "A Systematic Review of Mental Disorder, Suicide, and Deliberate Self-Harm in Lesbian, Gay and Bisexual People." *BMC Psychiatry* 8, no. 1 (2008): 70.

Kirby, T., and M. Thornber-Dunwell. "High-Risk Drug Practices Tighten Grip on London Gay Scene." *Lancet* 381, no. 9861 (January 2013): 101–102.

Klaar, C. M. "Straight Wives of HIV-Positive Husbands Who Contracted the Virus Through Male-to-Male Sexual Contact." *Journal of GLBT Family Studies* 8, no. 1 (2012): 99–120.

Kruks, G. "Gay and Lesbian Homeless/Street Youth: Special Issues and Concerns." *Journal of Adolescent Health* 12, no. 7 (Nov. 1991): 515–18.

Kwon, Paul. *Resilience in Lesbian, Gay and Bisexual Individuals.* Pullman USA, 2013.

Laing, Olivia. *The Trip to Echo Spring: On Writers and Drinking.* 2014.

Lanier, Jaron. *Who Owns the Future?* . Simon & Schuster, 2014.

Lee, Rita. "Health Care Problems of Lesbian, Gay, Bisexual, and Transgender Patients." *Western Journal of Medicine* 172, no. 6 (June 2000): 403–408.

Leserman, Jane. "Sexual Abuse History: Prevalence, Health Effects, Mediators, and Psychological Treatment." *Psychosomatic Medicine* 67, no. 6 (November/December 2005): 906–15.

Levinthal, Charles. *Drugs, Behavior, and Modern Society.* Massachusetts: Pearson Education, Inc., 1996.

Ling, Murtaugh K, Krishnamurti T, Reback CJ, Shoptaw, S. "Spend today, Clean Tomorrow: Predicting Methamphetamine Abstinence in a Randomized Controlled Trial." *Health Psychology*, September 2013: 958–66.

Lloyd, Shane, and Don Operario. "HIV Risk among Men Who Have Sex with Men Who Have Experienced Childhood Sexual Abuse: Systematic Review and Meta-Analysis." *AIDS Education and Prevention* 24, no. 3 (2012): 228–41.

Marshal, Michael P., Mark S. Friedman, Ron Stall, et al. "Sexual Orientation and Adolescent Substance Use: A Meta-Analysis and Methodological Review." 103, no. 4 (2008): 546–556.

Marshal, Mark P., Mark S. Friedman, Ron Stall, K. M. King, J. Miles, M. A. Gold, O. G. Bukstein, and J. Q. Morse. "Sexual Orientation and Adolescent Substance Use: A Meta-Analysis and Methodological Review." *Addiction* 103, no. 4 (2008): 546–56.

Miller, Lisa. "The Trans-Everything CEO." *New York*, September 2014: 8–21.

Minichiello, V., R. Mariño1, J. Browne, M. Jamieson, K. Peterson, B. Reuter, and K. Robinson. "A Profile of the Clients of Male Sex Workers in Three Australian Cities." *Australian and New Zealand Journal of Public Health* 23, no. 5 (October 1999): 511–18.

Mustanski, Brian S., Robert Garofalo, and Erin M. Emerson. "Mental Health Disorders, Psychological Distress, and Suicidality in a Diverse Sample of Lesbian, Gay, Bisexual, and Transgender Youths." *AJPH* 100 (December 2010): 2426–32.

Newton, Joseph E. O., W. Brian McPherson, Peggy T. Ackerman, Jerry G. Jones, and Roscoe A Dykman. "Prevalence of Post-Traumatic Stress Disorder and Other Psychiatric Diagnoses in Three Groups of Abused Children (Sexual, Physical, and Both)." *Child Abuse and Neglect* 22, no. 8 (August 1998): 759–74.

Nodin, N., P. Valera, A. Ventuneac, E. Maynard, and A. Carballo-Diéguez. "The Internet Profiles of Men Who Have Sex with Men within Bareback Websites." *Culture, Health & Sexuality* 13, no. 9 (2011): 1015–29.

Peredaa, Noemí, Georgina Guilerab, Maria Fornsa, and Juana Gómez-Benitob. "The Prevalence of Child Sexual Abuse in Community and Student Samples: A Meta-analysis." *Clinical Psychology Review* 29, no. 4 (June 2009): 328–38.

Phillips, Michael, and Shirley Wang. "US Veterans Try New Ways To Heal the Wounds of War." *The Wall Street Journal*, September 14, 2014.

Ramirez-Valles, J., Y. Molina, J. Dirkes "Stigma towards PLWHA: The Role of Internalized Homosexual Stigma in Latino Gay/Bisexual Male and Transgender Communities." *AIDS Education and Prevention* 25, no. 3 (2013): 179–89.

Reback, C., and S. Larkins. "HIV Risk Behaviors among a Sample of Heterosexually Identified Men Who Occasionally Have Sex with Another Mane and/or a Trans-woman." *Journal of Sex Research* 50, no. 2 (2013): 151–63.

Remafedi, Gary. "Male Homosexuality: The Adolescent's Perspective." *Pediatrics* 79, no. 3 (March 1987): 326–30.

Russell, S. T., T. J. Clarke, and J. Clary. "Are Teens 'Post-Gay'? Contemporary Adolescents' Sexual Identity Labels." *Journal of Youth and Adolescence* 38, no. 7 (August 2009): 884–90.

Saewyc, Elizabeth, Carol Skay, Kimberly Richens, Elizabeth Reis, Colleen Poon, and Aileen Murphy. "Sexual Orientation, Sexual Abuse, and HIV-Risk Behaviors among Adolescents in the Pacific Northwest." *American Journal of Public Health* 96, no. 6 (June 2006): 1104–10.

Shoptaw,S., R. Weiss, B. Munjas, C. Hucks-Ortiz, S. Young, S. Larkins, G. Victorianne, and P. Gorbach. "Homonegativity, Substance Use, Sexual Risk Behaviors, and HIV Status in Poor and Ethnic Men Who Have Sex with Men in Los Angeles." *Journal of Urban Health* 86, suppl. 1 (July 2009): 77.

Stall, Ron, Thomas Mills, John Williamson, et al. ". Association of Co-occurring Psychosocial Health Problems and Increased Vulnerability to HIV/AIDS Among Urban Men Who Have Sex With Men." *American Journal of Public Health* 93, no. 6 (June 2003) 939–42.

Schulte, Paul. *Cravings for Deliverance.* New York: Lantern Press, 2014.

Starks, T. J., H. J. Rendina, A. S. Breslow, J. T. Parson, and S. A. Golub. "The Psychological Cost of Anticipating HIV Stigma for HIV-Negative Gay and Bisexual Men." *AIDS and Behavior* 17, no. 8 (2013): 2732–41.

Tucker, Patrick. "The Military Is Building Brain Chips to Treat PTSD." *Defense One Newsletter*, May 25, 2014.

Twerski, Abraham. *Addictive Thinking: Understanding Self-decdption.* 2nd edition. Hazelden, 1997.

Wilson, Bill. 12 Steps and Twelve Traditions. New York, 1952.

Wang, Gene-Jack, Nora D. Volkow, Linda Chang, Eric Miller, et al. "Partial Recovery of Brain Metabolism in Methamphetamine Abusers After Protracted Abstinence." *American Journal of Psychiatry* 161 (2004): 242–8.

Wang, J. C., A. L. Hinrichs, H. Stock, et al. "Evidence of Common and Specific Genetic Effects: Association of the Muscarinic Acetylcholine Receptor M2 (CHRM2) Gene with Alcohol Dependence and Major Depressive Syndrome." *Human Molecular Genetics* 13, no. 17 (2004): 1903–11.

Whitfield, Charles. *A Gift to Myself.* Florida: Health Communications, 1990.

Index